CH00920043

Tom Holland is th
which won the Hessen
was shortlisted for the Samuel Johnson Prize, *Persian Fire*, *Millennium*, *In the Shadow of the Sword* and, most recently, *Dynasty*. His translation of Herodotus' *Histories* was published by Penguin Classics in 2013.

TOM HOLLAND

Athelstan

The Making of England

PENGUIN BOOKS

PENGUIN BOOKS

UK | USA | Canada | Ireland | Australia
India | New Zealand | South Africa

Penguin Books is part of the Penguin Random House group of companies
whose addresses can be found at global.penguinrandomhouse.com.

First published by Allen Lane 2016
First published in Penguin Books 2018
003

Set in 9.5/13.5 pt Sabon LT Std
Typeset by Jouve (UK), Milton Keynes
Printed and bound in Great Britain by Clays Ltd, Elcograf S.p.A.

ISBN: 978-0-141-98733-0

www.greenpenguin.co.uk

Contents

To Ned and Daisy, children of Wessex

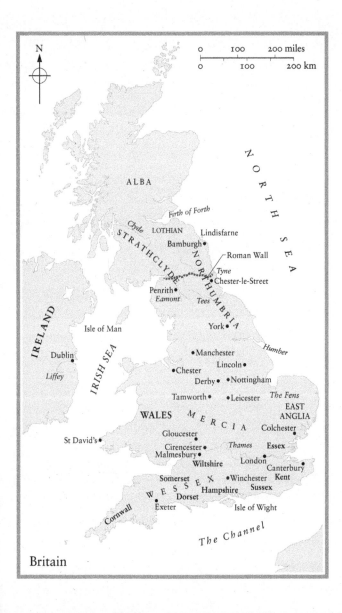

Britain

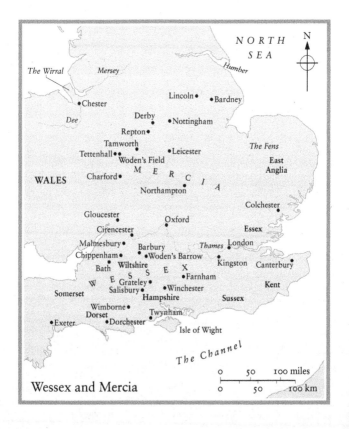

NORTH
SEA

N

The Wirral
Mersey
Humber

•Chester
Lincoln• •Bardney
Dee
Derby •Nottingham
Repton•
Tamworth
Tettenhall•• •Leicester
The Fens
Woden's Field
East
Anglia
M E R C I A
WALES Charford•
Northampton

Colchester•
Gloucester•
Cirencester• Oxford•
Essex
Malmesbury• Barbury Thames London•
Chippenham• •Woden's Barrow
Bath Wiltshire S Kingston• Canterbury•
W E S E X
•Grateley •Farnham
Kent
Somerset Salisbury• •Winchester
Hampshire Sussex
Wimborne•
Dorset Twynham
•Exeter •Dorchester
Isle of Wight

The Channel

0 50 100 miles
0 50 100 km

Wessex and Mercia

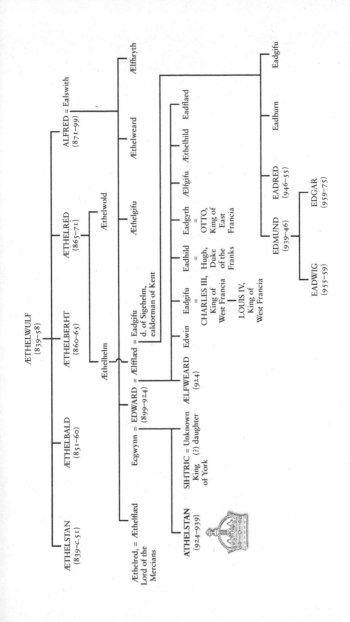

Athelstan

Brunanburh

It was the most terrible conflict that anyone could remember. Entire kingdoms were mobilized for combat. Slaughter fit to stupefy poets was visited on the ranks of the rival combatants. The memory of it would long endure. Some forty years after the churned mud of the battlefield had returned to grass, and despite the passing of the generation which had fought it, the commemorations persisted. Not merely a war, it was enshrined as something altogether more devastating: as the 'Great War'.[1]

'*Æðelstan cyning lædde fyrde to Brunanbyrig*': 'Athelstan the king led the levy to Brunanburh.'[2] Nine hundred and thirty-seven years had passed since the birth of Christ. For the first time, a single king laid claim to the whole of Britain. The heartland of Athelstan's realm was to be found in the south of the island, in the ancient kingdom of Wessex, which by the time of his accession in AD 924 had come to stretch from Cornwall to Kent. At his coronation, though, he had been crowned as the king not of the West Saxons, but of the Anglo-Saxons: due reflection of the fact that the Angles of Mercia, who inhabited the lands immediately north of Wessex, were his subjects too.[3] Then, in 927, Athelstan had ridden past the River

3

Humber and entered York. Princes in the lands beyond the city, intimidated by the scope of his power, had scrabbled to acknowledge his authority. Never before had the grasp of a southern king reached so far. Wessex, Mercia and now Northumbria: all the peoples who spoke the conqueror's own language, the whole way to the Firth of Forth, acknowledged Athelstan as their lord. In mark of this, he adopted a splendid and fateful new title, that of '*Rex Anglorum*': 'King of the English'. Athelstan's horizons, though, were wider still. His ambitions were not content with the rule of the English alone. He aspired to be acknowledged as lord of the entire island: by the inhabitants of the various kingdoms of the Welsh, and by the Welsh-speaking Cumbrians of Strathclyde, whose kings held sway from the Clyde down to the Roman Wall, and by the Scots, who lived beyond the Forth in the highland realm of Alba. All had duly been obliged to bow their necks to him. In May 934, when Constantin, the King of the Scots, briefly attempted defiance, Athelstan led an army deep into Alba and put its heartlands to the torch. Constantin was quickly brought to heel. Humbly he acknowledged the invader as his overlord. When poets and chroniclers hailed Athelstan as '*rex totius Britanniae*' – 'the king of the whole of Britain' – they were not indulging in idle flattery, but simply stating fact.

Britain, though, was not the world. The seas that washed the island were a menace as well as a moat. For a hundred years and more, they had borne on their tides war-fleets bristling with pirates from pagan lands. Scandinavia, a land so lost to cold and darkness that there was reportedly nothing for its inhabitants to do during the long winter months save to rut and breed, had long been notorious as 'the womb of nations'.[4] Its young men, hungry for land and contemptuous of the Christian faith, had found in the monasteries and kingdoms of Britain irresistibly rich pickings. '*Wicingas*', their victims called them: 'robbers'. Altars had been stripped bare of all their fittings, and kings bled of their treasure. Then, when there was nothing else left to take, the *Wicingas* – the 'Vikings' – had moved in for the kill. In succession, the proud and venerable kingdoms of Northumbria and Mercia had been hewn to pieces. Only the resolution of Athelstan's grandfather, a shrewd and indomitable warrior-king named Alfred, had prevented Wessex from succumbing to an identical fate. Gradually, inexorably, bloodily, the fight had been taken to the Vikings. Strongholds lost decades previously to native rule had been won back. Athelstan's conquest of York, as well as securing him the sway of Northumbria, had also terminated its rule by a lengthy sequence of Viking potentates. Britain seemed buttressed at last against the predations of the heathen.

But that was to reckon without the treachery of Constantin. In 927, he and rulers from across the island were obliged by Athelstan to swear publicly that they would never have dealings with idol worship: an oath calculated to remind them of their solemn duty as Christian kings. A decade on, though, collusion with the heathen proved a temptation impossible for Constantin to resist. Across the Irish Sea, in the Viking stronghold of Dublin, a warlord by the name of Olaf Guthfrithsson had long had his eyes fixed on York – a city which, until its capture by Athelstan, had been held by his family. Just as Constantin yearned to cast off the yoke of his subordination, so Olaf dreamed of recovering his patrimony. It was a potent meeting of interests. By 937, the alliance was out in the open. That autumn, Constantin marched south. With him rode Owain, the King of Strathclyde. Meanwhile, at the head of an immense war-fleet, Olaf made the crossing from Ireland to join them. The combined armies of the three leaders, two of them the most powerful kings in Britain after Athelstan himself, and the third a notorious warlord, represented a potentially mortal threat to the nascent English realm. Abruptly, after a rise to greatness so dazzling as to have illumined the northern ocean with its brilliance, its future seemed menaced by shadow. Athelstan, brought the news, was numbed at first by the sheer scale of the calamity that threatened all his labours. Then, with a supreme effort of will, he geared himself for the great confrontation that he knew he could not duck. What option was there, in the final reckoning, save to ride and confront the invaders head on?

At stake, though, was not just the future of Athelstan's kingdom. Beyond the world of men, in skies and lonely forests, the shudder of the looming battle was also being felt. As the King of the English rode northwards, the numbers in his train swelling with his advance, ravens as well as warriors began to follow in his wake.[5] The birds were notorious creatures of ill omen: clamorous, untrustworthy, hungry for human flesh. Once, many generations previously, the English had believed that the raven was endowed with the gift of augury; but then, brought into the light of Christ, they had come to understand better. 'How is a senseless bird to foretell the future of men reborn and baptised into the image of God?'[6] In the ranks of the heathen, though, where its image was often to be seen embroidered on vaunting battle-standards, there were many who attended to its speech. Just as twin ravens sat at the ears of Odin, the Vikings' greatest god, and told him 'tidings of all that they saw or heard',[7] so on battlefields were the birds known to serve their favourites as prophets of victory. This superstition, for all that the English had long since been redeemed from it, could not entirely be ignored. To march armed for battle and hear overhead the flocking of ravens was indeed to know that a time of slaughter was near. It was sufficient to perturb the warriors of even the most Christ-blessed king.

The blaze of Athelstan's glory, for all its unexampled radiance, could not entirely illumine the realm of shadow in which the workings of witchcraft flourished. The powers of necromancy which might be invoked by a heathen warrior were fearsome things. Invulnerability against the biting of iron; the fettering with paralysis of an enemy, so that he would find it impossible to lift his sword; weapons that sang in the heat of battle, with a loud and ringing sound: all these were treasured by the pagans as gifts from Odin. The surest mark of the god's favour, though, lay not in charms but in a ferocity so terrible as to render those possessed by it bestial. 'Wolfskin-wearers they are called, who bear bloody shields in the slaughter; they redden spears when they join the fighting.'[8] Willingly these shape-shifters surrendered themselves in their savagery to the power of demons. As they howled and ran in packs at their prey, so would they see the battlefield swept by a warp of blood.

> The fabric is threaded
> with men's intestines
> and firmly weighted
> with men's heads.[9]

To combat warriors possessed by such a fighting frenzy, to stand firm against them, solid in a shield-wall and never yielding ground, was to meet in battle as well the fiends whom the Vikings, in their folly and their superstition, enshrined as gods. Here, for Athelstan, 'a man so devout as to be famed for it across the wide globe',[10] was a reflection fit to steel him even more implacably for the death-struggle that lay ahead. As his army approached Brunanburh, and scouts reported the presence ahead of the teeming hordes of his foes, he knew that more than the fate of men was hanging in the balance. Demons as well, those who spoke through ravens or gave to their followers the speed and the iron-jawed hunger of a wolf, were readying themselves for the slaughter that was to come.

Dawn broke. Battle was joined. As the sky above the rival armies lightened, so the field of Brunanburh began to darken red. All day long the work of killing lasted. Shafts sang, spears sped, swords were washed in blood. Shield-wall pushed against shield-wall – but in the end, as the sun began to sink in the West, it was those loyal to Athelstan, their lord, the ring-giver, who secured the victory. West

Saxons and men of Mercia, they broke their adversaries. Olaf and those of his entourage still standing turned and fled, pursued by bands of West Saxons; and then, on reaching their ships, pushed them frantically out into the sea. 'On the dark floodtide the king made his escape.'[11] Constantin too, 'that grey-haired warrior, the old deceitful one,'[12] lived to tell the tale of his defeat, slinking back to his highland fastnesses – but he left behind him on the field of Brunanburh his son. The young prince of Alba was not the only man of note to have fallen. Five kings lay amid the tangle of the dead, and seven of Olaf's earls, and countless multitudes besides. Athelstan's triumph had been bloodily secured.

That night, the howling of wolves maddened with excitement at their feast of carrion served as a mocking threnody for the delusions of the pagans. Men who had thought by means of sorcery to take on the form and ferocity of a wolf pack now themselves wetted lupine jaws. The ravens, flocking to the corpse-strewn mud of Brunanburh, fed greedily. If indeed it was true that before the battle they had given messages to the heathen, these stood revealed now as delusory. Few could fail to recognize in the victory the guiding hand of the Almighty, who had rewarded Athelstan for a lifetime of exemplary piety by permitting him to keep his kingdom intact. For a century and more, the Vikings had treated Britain as the ravens which now swooped and hopped across the battlefield were treating the fallen: as prey to be picked clean. The struggle to heal what might have become death wounds, to bind them up and to staunch the flow of blood, the great cause to which Athelstan's dynasty had devoted itself for three generations, had been decisively won. If the presence of Constantin and Owain in arms against the *rex Anglorum* served as a reminder that in the northern reaches of Britain there were still those who defied his supremacy, then there could no doubting the loyalty of his Anglo-Saxon subjects. Brunanburh had been won by the men of Wessex and Mercia fighting together side by side; and now, with York secured against the attempt of Olaf to wrest it back, Northumbria too remained a part of Athelstan's realm. The outlines of a new and potentially enduring state, rendered that much clearer by the decisive result of the battle, had begun to emerge.

True, there remained debate as to what this agglomeration of ancient kingdoms, now joined under the rule of a single king, should properly be termed. '*Saxonia*', some suggested: 'Saxonland'. There were others, though, beyond the reaches of Wessex, who preferred the obvious alternative: '*Anglia*'. Sure enough, it was this name, in the wake of Brunanburh, which increasingly won out. A few generations on from the 'Great War', men looking back at it could see in the terrible battle the birth pangs of an entire new order, in which 'all the fields of Britain were joined as one, and everywhere there was peace, and prosperity was general'.[13] Athelstan, the great conqueror who had secured this happy result, was commemorated as the founder of something glorious and new: the united kingdom of what, in the native language of those who lived in it, was coming to be known as 'Englalonde'.

'Never on this island before such killing.' The forging of

England, to those who in the generations which followed Brunanburh looked back in wonder at Athelstan's victory, was an achievement so great, so formidable, so momentous that only in the context of centuries could it properly be appreciated. The kingship of the English, startling innovation though it was, had not emerged from nowhere. The blood spilled by Athelstan's warriors at Brunanburh, for all that it had served as the cement of the new monarchy, was hardly the first shed by the Saxons or the Angles to have wetted British soil. Only the scale of the slaughter had rendered it exceptional. The story which had reached its climax at Brunanburh had venerable beginnings. 'Never before were so many felled by the edges of swords – no, not since from the east the Angles and Saxons, as we are told in ancient books full of wisdom, landed after sailing the broad seas, landed in their quest for Britain.'[14]

The roots of the monarchy founded by Athelstan reached a long way back indeed.

I
Wessex

'Not since from the east the Angles and Saxons, as we are told in ancient books full of wisdom, landed after sailing the broad seas, landed in their quest for Britain . . . '

Without tradition there could be no innovation. The extraordinary labour of state-creation performed by Athelstan, his father and his grandfather, on a scale unprecedented in British history though it was, depended for its legitimacy on sanctions derived from the past. The claim of a single monarchy to the rule of the whole of Britain could not possibly depend upon force alone. Alfred, in his desperate and ultimately triumphant struggle to stave off the ruin of his kingdom, had marshalled scribes as well as spearmen. The royal household into which Athelstan was born in either 894 or 895 was not lacking in 'ancient books full of wisdom'. The young boy, as he grew up, would have been left in no doubt as to the antiquity and achievements of the dynasty to which he belonged.

Scholars learned in the details of Britain's eventful history had placed the founding of the West Saxon royal line in the broadest possible context, that of the numerous migrations and invasions which had marked the island's past. First, crossing the Channel, had come its original inhabitants, the Britons; then, landing in its northernmost reaches after being swept there by storms, a barbarously tattooed people from Scythia known as the Picts; and then the Romans. For centuries, much of the island had lain under the rule of the Caesars; and during that time they had raised numerous markers of their greatness. 'The cities they built, the forts, the bridges and the streets, were all of them wonderfully fashioned – as can still be seen to this day.'[1] One emperor, by the name of Severus, even built a wall, 'stretching from sea to sea, for the protection of the Britons'.[2] The time came, though, after four centuries of rule by the Romans, when their greatness began to crumble and they were no longer able to maintain their defence of Britain. The Picts, who had lurked unconquered beyond the great wall built by Severus, now flooded southwards and inflicted terrible slaughter. When the Romans, beset by invasions of their own, refused to come to the rescue, the Britons in their despair and misery turned for assistance to mercenaries from across the North Sea. Entire tribes began to migrate. One of these was named the Angles, another the Saxons, and a third the Jutes.

Right from the beginning, then, the adventurers who had sailed for Britain half a millennium before the time of Athelstan had been joined in a common destiny. This, to a child growing up in the court of King Alfred, was a manifest truth. Manifest to him as well was the hand of the Almighty in the turn of events by which the newcomers had ended up displacing their employers, and taking possession of much of Britain. Just as God had sent the Assyrians as tools of his wrath against His Chosen People, the Children of Israel, so had He found in the Angles, the Saxons and the Jutes a rod with which to punish the Britons. The offences of the native inhabitants of the island had, on their own confession, smelled to heaven. Drunkenness, idolatry, violence – not a depravity, but they had revelled in it. 'And so the fire of righteous justice, ignited by this history of criminality, blazed from sea to sea.'[3] The immigrants, after expelling the Picts back beyond the Roman Wall, had been prompted by the treachery and self-evident cowardice of the Britons to turn on their hosts. The leaders of tiny warbands, blessed as only the agents of divine purpose could be, had succeeded in carving out for themselves entire kingdoms. And among their number had been the ancestor of Athelstan.

Cerdic, so it was recorded, had arrived in Britain 495 years after the birth of Christ. He had sailed there from the land of the Saxons in command of five boats. Landing on the south coast, he and his son Cynric had promptly embarked on what was to prove a most successful campaign of conquest. Centuries on, the record of their battle honours was still lovingly preserved at the West Saxon court: Charford, Salisbury, Barbury. These victories were only the first of many redounding to the glory of the house of Wessex. Cerdic's talent for defeating Britons and killing their leaders had been amply inherited by his heirs. In 577, no fewer than three British kings had been eliminated in a single battle fought just to the north of Bath. Bath itself, Cirencester, Gloucester: all had fallen to the invaders. A century on from Cerdic's arrival in Britain, Saxon arms had reached the Bristol Channel. The immigrants had become the rulers; the natives the aliens. '*Wealas*', or 'foreigners', the Britons were derisively termed by their conquerors: 'Welsh'. The judgement of the heavens on their sins had been clear.

Such, at any rate, was the story told at the court of Athelstan's grandfather to explain the origins of the West Saxon monarchy. To Alfred, both his line of unbroken descent from the venerable figure of Cerdic and the sheer antiquity of his kingdom were causes of great pride. Yet even in the library of books compiled under his patronage, there were tantalizing hints of a rather different story. The earliest history of the English-speaking peoples, written by a monk named Bede a century and a half before the time of Alfred, made no mention of Cerdic. No small flotilla of ships, no landing on the south coast. The kingdom of Wessex, it seemed, had not always been Wessex. The West Saxons, Bede implied, had originally been known as the Gewisse. Scholars in the time of Alfred took differing perspectives on this intriguing detail. One, embarking on the first translation of Bede from Latin into English, simply excised all references to it; but a second, a monk from St David's named Asser, observed in a biography he wrote of Alfred that the Welsh still called the West Saxons 'Gewisse'. Asser, as a Welshman himself, and one who had ended up a bishop in Wessex, might equally have pointed out that Cerdic, the founder of the West Saxon royal line, had a name that, far from being English, was actually Welsh. So too did several other of his immediate heirs. 'How little can we know,' Alfred reflected, 'concerning what was before our time, except through memory and inquiry.'[4] Yet memory and inquiry could both fail those who relied upon them. That the line of Cerdic might originally have been as British as it was Saxon, and that a kingdom recognizable as Wessex might not have been planted in the immediate wake of the landing of his ships, but instead have emerged gradually from a whole swirl of influences, both native and immigrant: here were possibilities that few at Alfred's court had any incentive to consider. The West Saxon monarchy had no interest in tracing its lineage back to the defeated Britons. Its origins ultimately had to derive from a distant and heroic Germanic past, or it was nothing.

The tracing of such an ancestry did not come without cost, though. Although the role played by the West Saxon monarchy in the fulfilment of God's plans was evident for all to see, the fact that He had permitted the house of Cerdic to disinherit the Britons did not alter one glaring and awkward fact: that its earliest kings had all been pagan. The terrifying god worshipped by the Vikings as Odin had been known by the ancestors of Athelstan as Woden – and enshrined by them as their forefather. Other pagan dynasties in England had invariably done the same. Rare was the royal genealogy that had not borne witness to the fecundity of Woden. Seen from the perspective of a later age, one illumined by the light of Christ, there could be little doubt as to who should be blamed for this monstrous conceit. The fault, so it was generally agreed, had lain less with the pagans themselves than with the Britons. No one had been more influential in pressing this argument than Bede. Among all their many other unspeakable crimes, he argued, one in particular had roused divine anger against the Britons: 'that they never preached the Faith to the Saxons or Angles who dwelt with them in Britain'. The consequence was that for many generations much of the island had been lost to heathendom. 'But God in His goodness did not utterly abandon the people whom He had chosen; for He remembered them.'[5] From Rome, a pope named Gregory had sent a mission to convert the pagans of Britain. It had landed in Kent, in 597. A Roman monk had been enthroned as archbishop in Canterbury. Gradually, over the course of the following century, kingdom after kingdom had been brought to acknowledge Christ. Woden, no longer worshipped as a god, had suffered a signal demotion. Although he remained enshrined in the genealogy of the house of Cerdic, he did so merely as 'a barbarian king'.[6] Athelstan never had any cause to feel diminished by this recalibration. Just the opposite. He knew, as only someone brought up in a court famed for its piety could do, just how much better it was to rule as a servant of Christ than the descendant of a god.

Which said, the role played by the kings of Wessex in the conversion of England to the Christian faith had not been as glorious as it might have been. The devotion of the West Saxons to their ancient gods had been fierce. It was noted by one chronicler writing in Alfred's reign that in the very year of Gregory's elevation to the papacy much blood had been spilled in Wessex beside an ancient haunt of demons. 'Great slaughter was made at Woden's barrow.'[7] The contrast with the Kentish kingdom, which had welcomed the mission sent by Gregory, and duly been rewarded with an archbishop, was glaring. More burnished yet was the example of Northumbria. There, during the first decades of its existence as a Christian kingdom, saints of astonishing holiness and potency had blazed an example that still, centuries on, remained as radiant as ever. Some, such as Cuthbert, a monk as loved for the quality of his miracles and his generosity to the poor as he was admired for the formidable calibre of his austerities, had yearned for the life of a hermit, and steadily retreated to ever lonelier and more inaccessible spots; but others had been kings.

Oswald, 'a man beloved of God',[8] offered a young prince like Athelstan a particularly pertinent role model. The exiled son of a fallen Northumbrian king, he had won back his patrimony in heroically Christ-fearing style. In AD 634, cornered in a field beside the Roman Wall and facing massive odds, he had raised a wooden cross, loudly affirmed his faith before the serried ranks of his followers, and then gone on to secure a glorious victory. As puissant a warrior as he was a devout patron of the Church, Oswald had ruled for eight triumphant years, and come to be hailed – in admittedly exaggerated terms – as 'Emperor of all Britain'.[9] When he finally died in battle, defeated and hacked to pieces by a pagan king of Mercia, it had been as a martyr. Almost half a century later, after the Mercians in their turn had become Christian, portions of Oswald's dismembered body had been laid to rest near Lincoln, in a monastery named Bardney. On the night before their inhumation, an eerie beam of light had been seen rising from the coffin into the sky. Numerous other miracles had followed. Fevers were cured and evil spirits banished. Similar wonders were attributed to Oswald's head, which, together with the uncorrupted body of Saint Cuthbert, ranked among the supreme treasures of Northumbria. Nor was it only in Britain that the relics of the martyr king were spoken of with awe. 'The rays of his beneficent light shone far overseas.'[10] Monks in Frisia, ignoring the evident fact that Oswald's skull was preserved in Northumbria, even went so far as to lay claim to the head themselves.

Such fame, when viewed from Wessex, could hardly help but serve to emphasize just how lacking in martyrs the house of Cerdic was. Again and again, during the century that followed Pope Gregory's mission to the English, the role of West Saxon kings had been to serve as foils to their more glamorous Northumbrian counterparts. In 626 one of them had sponsored an assassination attempt on the first king of Northumbria to accept baptism, and been roundly thrashed in battle following its failure: an early and telling demonstration of just how potent the Christian god might be in war. Sure enough, nine years later, a king of Wessex – Cynegils by name – had accepted baptism himself. Oswald had stood as his godfather. For the next fifty years, a succession of West Saxon kings had veered between loyalty to their ancient gods and to Christ. Typical of this ambivalence was a usurper by the name of Cædwalla, who had seized the throne in 685. Christian contemporaries had understandably regarded him with deep suspicion. Not only was he unbaptized, but he had returned to Wessex from an exile spent in the thick woods of Sussex – the groves of which were notorious as the haunt of pagans. Nevertheless, once on the throne Cædwalla had fallen heavily under the influence of Wilfrid, a charismatic

and thoroughly imperious Northumbrian saint. Inspired
by his mentor to make amends for his heathen past, Cædwalla had invaded the Isle of Wight, a Jutish kingdom even
more steeped in pagan practices than Sussex, and won it
for Christ with a near-genocidal display of brutality. Then,
laying down his crown in 688, he had set off for Rome,
there to receive baptism at the hands of the pope himself.
His death a few days later had marked a key turning point
in the history of Wessex. Never again would a West Saxon
ascend the throne with the taint of paganism still about
him. The house of Cerdic now ranked as securely Christian. Athelstan was born into a dynasty that could boast of
a devotion to Christ reaching back more than two centuries. Yet still there lingered a certain nagging anxiety: that
Wessex, compared to Kent or Northumbria, ranked as a
parvenu among Christian powers, and that the lineage of
its ruling house lacked the glory bestowed upon those of
other kingdoms by kings of the holiness of Oswald.

What, though, if the role of Athelstan's forebears in
God's plans had been of a greater significance than a mere
cursory glance at the history of Wessex might suggest? The
demotion of Woden from god to mortal had served to open
up exciting new vistas of possibility. Scholars at the West
Saxon court, eager to trace his ancestry back to Adam, had
seized upon one particularly intriguing aspect of his
genealogy. Woden, so it was recorded during Alfred's
reign, had been the great-great-great-great-great-great-
great-great-great-great-great-grandson of a man named
Sceaf.[11] Various stories were told of this enigmatic figure:
that as a child he had drifted in from the seas on an

otherwise empty boat; that he had been raised by those who found him; that he had ended up a great king. Now, though, thanks to the researches undertaken at Alfred's court, the truth could finally be told. Sceaf had been the son of Noah. That he failed to feature in the Bible was merely a detail. Unlike the three sons of Noah who did enjoy mentions in Holy Scripture, Sceaf had been born on the Ark itself. Growing up, he had fathered the line that would culminate in the West Saxon dynasty. The implication of this startling revelation was momentous: that the house of Wessex could boast a pedigree as exclusive as any in the world.

It was, for anyone born into it, a reflection fit to stir the blood. Athelstan, as a descendant of Cerdic, could know himself the heir to a conception of monarchy that fused the heroic traditions of the Saxons with a lineage that reached the entire way back to Adam. Yet even this was not the sum of the inheritance that the young prince, as a throne-worthy heir, an *'ætheling'*, enjoyed. The kingship of Wessex, forged amid warfare and sanctioned by an awesome line of descent, had come, by the time of Athelstan's birth, to lay claim to a potent moral purpose as well. 'Placed am I by God as king over His holy Mount Sion, for the purpose of teaching His will and His law.'[12] Alfred's rendering of the Psalms into English, one of a number of translations which he attempted, served him as a mirror in which he could see reflected his own purposes and obligations. This conceit, vainglorious as it might have seemed in a ruler of lesser achievement, spoke profoundly of the elevated conception of kingship to which, resolutely and heroically, he had been committed all his reign. It was no surprise that Alfred, 'a man in the invariable habit of listening daily to divine services and Mass,'[13] should have found such a comfort in the Psalms: for their author, so the Bible taught, had been both a warrior and a king as well as a poet. David, who had felled the Philistine giant Goliath, brought security to his people and devoted himself to the arts of peace, had always provided Christian kings with their readiest model. 'Success in warfare, yes – but also in wisdom.'[14] So Alfred, inspired by his lifelong devotion to the lessons taught by Holy Scripture, summed up his manifesto for effective kingship. There could be no doubting what God expected of a man set in rule over others; no doubting either that the penalty for failing Him, and for denying the people of a Christian land peace, and abundance, and justice, would be answered for amid the torments of hell.

Alfred's pagan forebears, ignorant of this awful truth, had been content to reign as warlords, and to point to their success in battle as the proof of their descent from a god. Those swaggering, Christ-scorning days were long since gone, of course – but not the conviction that to rule as a king was to be touched by a supernatural power. Sure evidence for this was to be found in the Bible itself. As a boy, David had been blessed by the wisest seer in Israel, and anointed with oil as a mark that one day he would become a king; 'and the Spirit of the Lord came mightily upon him from that day forward'.[15] Christian kings too, as a token of their sacral status, had come to accept anointment. The practice had originated in 751, in the land of the Franks, when an upstart king by the name of Pepin had been anointed at his coronation. Three years later, the pope himself had travelled to Paris and repeated the ritual, anointing both Pepin and his two sons. The oil used in the ceremony was of an awesome potency, sufficient to extinguish fires and cleanse the sea of demons, and the man touched by it ruled from that moment on 'gratia Dei' – 'by the grace of God'. Kings on the opposite side of the Channel, not surprisingly, had been quick to take note. The opportunity to imitate the Frankish monarchy, the greatest in Christendom, was too good to miss. Sure enough, in 781 a king of Mercia had arranged for his son to be anointed, just as Pepin's had been: the first known royal consecration in British history.

And Alfred too had been anointed. Such, at any rate, was the tale told many years after the event was supposed to have taken place: that as a young prince of four or five he had been sent by his father to Rome, and there been consecrated by the pope himself. Whatever the truth of the story, the aura that it bestowed on him of the Old Testament's most celebrated king was unmistakable: for just as David had been the youngest of his father's sons, so was Alfred. Certainly, there were few during his childhood who would have anticipated him succeeding to the throne of Wessex. Æthelwulf, Alfred's father, had provided his kingdom with no fewer than five *æthelings*: a total that, under normal circumstances, might have been expected to prove more than adequate. The circumstances, though, were not normal. It was a wind age, a wolf age. One after the other, Alfred's four brothers had ruled as king, then died; and it was as a lieutenant to the fourth of these, Æthelred, that Alfred had first made his mark in battle against the Vikings. The victory, though, had proven illusory. The pagans had soon returned, and in overwhelming force. The death of Æthelred soon after Easter in 871 had left Alfred the king of a realm confronting the gravest crisis of its existence. For seven years he had fought desperately to keep the invaders at bay. All the while, though, the shadows had continued to lengthen. Then, in 878, 'in mid-winter after Twelfth Night',[16] the descent of a Viking warband on the royal residence of Chippenham had left the very survival of Wessex hanging by a thread. Alfred, taken hopelessly by surprise, had fled to an island in Somerset so mired around by swamps as effectively to be impregnable; and there he had licked his wounds and prayed for guidance. Finally, four months after his flight from Chippenham, he had ventured back out from the marshes. God had kept watch over him. The invaders were defeated and scoured from Wessex; *burh*s – towns ringed about with fortifications and endowed with market-places for the generation of taxes – were planted along its frontiers; his subjects steeled for continued struggle. Just as David had saved his people from the Philistines, so had Alfred saved his from the Vikings. No wonder, then, looking back at his great feats, that his subjects should indeed have believed him consecrated from an early age to rule: literally touched by the divine.

Not every king, though, could be reckoned a second David. When Alfred succeeded his brother Æthelred in 871, it had been 'with the approval of divine will and according to the unanimous wish of all the inhabitants of the kingdom'[17] – a decision that had triumphantly been proven the correct one. Nevertheless, it had stored up problems. Æthelred had left behind him two young sons, Æthelhelm and Æthelwold – and although clearly, at the time of his death, it had been out of the question to entrust the future of Wessex to either of them, untested children that they were, the claim of Alfred's nephews to the throne could not merely be discounted. That Alfred himself had fathered two *æthelings*, Edward and Æthelweard, did not necessarily alter this. There was no accepted custom in Wessex which decreed that the son of a king was bound to succeed his father. Quite the opposite. Over the long course of West Saxon history, the throne had frequently passed from uncle to nephew, from brother to brother, from cousin to cousin. Alfred's father had been the first son of a king to succeed directly to the throne in almost two hundred years. Ultimately, it was the consensus of the great men of the kingdom, and the acclamation of the people, that served to raise an *ætheling* to the throne of Wessex and secure his legitimacy. Not even a ruler as admired as Alfred could take for granted that his eldest son would succeed him by right.

Nevertheless, more than any West Saxon king before him, he had won for himself the opportunity to influence what might happen after his death. 'King of the Saxons, unshakeable pillar of the people of the west, a man full of justice, active in war, learned in speech, and above all, instructed in divine learning':[18] these were qualifications that no one in Wessex could seriously dispute. As a result, despite the fact that Edward was younger than his two cousins, few were prepared to begrudge the evident favouritism with which Alfred treated his eldest son. When Æthelhelm and Æthelwold began openly to complain that their uncle had appropriated their inheritance, he spiked their capacity for mischief-making by summoning the chief men of Wessex and daring any of them to accuse him openly 'of treating my young kinsmen wrongfully, the older or the younger'.[19] None of them did. Then, capitalizing on his advantage, Alfred promptly made public his will. By its terms, Edward was granted a vast swathe of lands, stretching from the far west of Wessex the whole way to its eastern limits, which served very pointedly to entrench his authority across the entire kingdom. Æthelhelm and Æthelwold, meanwhile, had to rest content with a few scattered estates.

Had Edward proven unequal to the responsibilities laid upon his shoulders, then his two cousins would doubtless have found a ready opportunity to resurrect their cause; but he did not. In 893, when a vast force of Vikings, bloodied in battle against the Franks, crossed the Channel and sought to take their chance in Wessex, Alfred had sufficient confidence in his son to leave the handling of the principal onslaught to him. His trust turned out to be fully justified. Edward, falling on the invaders at Farnham, roundly defeated them, and then harried the survivors across the Thames. Further marks of his father's favour soon followed. By 898 Edward had come to be named in a charter issued in Kent as 'rex': 'king'. As so often, Alfred was smoothing the way to the future by paying homage to the past. Only during the reign of his grandfather had the Kentish people come definitively under the rule of the house of Cerdic; and a ghostly sense of Wessex and Kent as separate kingdoms still lingered in the minds of many. Yet Alfred's willingness to grant Edward the title to what had once been an independent kingdom was not primarily about flattering the sensibilities of his Kentish subjects. Rather, it served as the culminating manoeuvre in what had been a long and painstaking campaign: to enshrine at the heart of the West Saxon monarchy the convention that a father be succeeded by his son.

Which in turn, of course, had major implications for Edward's eldest: Athelstan. The first-born son of Alfred's first-born son was a boy clearly destined for great things; and yet he was raised, for all that, under the shadow of an irony. Edward's determination to secure the throne for himself as his father's heir risked not solidifying his own child's prospects, but undermining them. Athelstan's mother, a noblewoman named Ecgwynn, ranked as a mere pawn in the great game of the West Saxon royal succession. No matter what the charms that had persuaded Edward to take her to bed, she had brought him little dynastic advantage. Her status at court, amid the turbulent currents of its various rivalries, was precarious. So too, as a result, was Athelstan's. Certainly, he could not rely upon his father to promote his fortunes in the way that Edward was able to depend upon Alfred. With the succession to the old king not yet fully secured, it was out of the question to bestow on the young *ætheling* anything that might approximate to a rank as the heir apparent. Ecgwynn might need to be sacrificed at any moment. The odds against Athelstan ever becoming king were considerable.

Yet if Edward was content to regard his eldest son with a determinedly calculating eye, there was another at the West Saxon court who looked on him with an altogether more transparent fondness. Alfred, who throughout his reign had combined martial prowess with a love of learning and a profound, not to say anxious, sense of Christian duty, seems to have discovered in the boy a mirror held up to his own long-distant childhood. Although he did not – as the pope was said to have done to him – consecrate Athelstan with oil, Alfred did grace his grandson with other honours that echoed those granted him when he, as a small boy himself, had visited Rome. 'We have decorated him, as a spiritual son, with the dignity of the *cingulum* and the vestments of the consulate.'[20] So the pope, writing to Alfred's father, had reported the details of the ceremony. Both the gifts bestowed on the young boy were fabulously ancient badges of power. A *cingulum* was the military belt that officers, back in the heyday of the Caesars, had worn as a marker of their rank; 'vestments of the consulate' the robes worn by those who, over the course of long centuries before as well as after the birth of Christ, had held the pre-eminent magistracy in the Roman state. Clearly, the impact of these awesome tokens of papal favour had stayed with Alfred all his life. Now, many decades on, he invested his grandson as he had once been invested in Rome: with a sword-belt and a richly dyed cloak. Those who marked the ceremony were left in no doubt as to its significance. One, a scholar learned in the language and imagery of power, was quick to make allusion to the consecration of David as a young boy, and to salute Athelstan with a sonorous epithet derived from ancient Rome: *'triumvir'*.[21]

Traditions drawn from the Bible and from the monarchy of the Caesars: both, by the end of Alfred's long reign, had come to be fused with the West Saxon conception of kingship. As Alfred himself had so momentously demonstrated, it took a special order of man to shoulder such a burdensome responsibility, and prove himself equal to it. That he had so publicly bestowed on his young grandson proofs of his favour reflected not merely his hopes for Athelstan, but his recognition of just how dependent was the future of Wessex on the quality of those who might follow him onto the throne. Redeemed as it had been from the brink of utter ruin, its frontiers now seemed sufficiently proof against the depredations of the Vikings that it was possible to imagine his heirs taking the fight to their foes, and advancing the limits of their kingdom beyond those of Wessex itself. Already, some of Alfred's more enthusiastic courtiers had begun to hail their lord as 'Ruler of all the Christians of the Island of Britain'.[22] The challenge for those who followed him would be to see if such hyperbolic terms might in any way be matched to reality. It went without saying, though, that all that lay in the lap and the favour of God. Whether Alfred's successors could prove themselves capable of building on his legacy – let alone what role, if any, Athelstan might grow up to play in the future of Britain – only time would tell.

2
Mercia

Over the course of Alfred's reign, kingship in Wessex had come to wear an impressive aspect. The sheer length of time he had spent on the throne; the heroic quality of his achievements; the aura of the sacral that clung to him as an anointed king: all had combined to endow him with a rare and potent prestige. Alfred had no illusions, though, as to the true basis of his power. Ultimately, it was not the praise of chroniclers or the rituals of the Church that made someone a king of Wessex, but his acceptance by the great men of the kingdom, the 'ealdormen', as their lord. It was because Alfred understood this that he had gone to such lengths to entrust his eldest son with both lands and responsibilities. Estates had brought Edward wealth, which enabled him to display generosity to those whose support he needed; military commands had given him experience in war, without which no king could hope to maintain his rule. When Alfred finally died in the autumn of 899, 'six days before All Saints' Day',[1] Edward could bury him knowing that his father, as befitted a man renowned for his love of learning, had given him the best possible apprenticeship.

Nothing, though, could be taken for granted. Over the

long course of West Saxon history, dynastic feuding had repeatedly taken a violent turn upon the death of a king. So it did again now. Despite the fact that Edward's election by the chief men of the kingdom was a foregone conclusion, not everyone rejoiced at the prospect of his reign. Even though Æthelhelm, the elder son of King Æthelred, had died a few years earlier, Æthelwold, his younger son, was still very much on the scene.[2] Determined as he was to lay claim to what he saw as his birthright, long kept from him by Alfred, the election of Edward only rendered him the more desperate. Accordingly, resolved to take his chance while the new king was still finding his feet, he launched a bold and despairing strike. His first move was to make as public a repudiation of his uncle as he could. Alfred, more than any of his predecessors, had made a point of condemning the sexual assault of women, and nuns especially; but Æthelwold, breaking into an abbey, flaunted his scorn for the dead king's law code by abducting one of the sisters and making her his wife.[3] The real marker of his rebellion, though, came with his seizure of two royal estates: Twynham in Hampshire and Wimborne in Dorset. Both lay in the south of the kingdom; and Wimborne in particular constituted a key strategic point. As well as providing whoever controlled it with ready access to both the north and the west of Wessex, it boasted an abbey, complete with readily defensible stone walls, and the tomb of Æthelred, Æthelwold's father. A stronghold ideally placed, then, it might have seemed, to serve the rebel prince as his capital.

Except that Edward, brought the news of his cousin's

insurrection, had no intention of allowing him to dig in. He could recognize Æthelwold's move for what it was: a potentially lethal emulation of his kingdom's deadliest foes. The seizure and fortification of a royal estate, the ravaging of the neighbourhood, the calculated attempt to demonstrate that a king was impotent to defend his lands and his people: all were favourite tactics of the Vikings. Edward, newly raised to the throne though he might be, was already seasoned enough a campaigner to know the value of speed. Accordingly, he made as fast as he could for Dorset. With him he took a force so intimidating that when he camped with it on an ancient hill fort outside Wimborne, Æthelwold had no choice but to accept that his bluff has been called. Just as many a cornered Viking had done before him, he waited until nightfall, then took to horseback and fled. Although a posse was sent by Edward in hot pursuit, Æthelwold had too much of a head start to be caught. Heading northwards, he crossed from Wessex into Mercia. Dark rumours were soon being reported of his ultimate destination. It was said that he had joined the Vikings in what once had been the Christian realm of Northumbria – and that he had been accepted by them as their king. Horrifyingly, it was even whispered that he had abandoned his faith in Christ. A Viking warlord with the blood of the royal house of the West Saxons in his veins: here, despite Edward's success in expelling him from Wessex, was a potentially mortal threat.

Meanwhile, for Athelstan, the consequences of the crisis in relations between his father and Æthelwold were as immediate as they were unsettling. The divisions in the royal household were too menacing for Edward not to attempt to bandage them up. Much as his cousin had signalled his rebellion with a marriage, so the new king chose to assert his own authority over the house of Wessex by taking a new wife: a niece of Æthelwold by the name of Ælfflæd.[4] Ecgwynn, Athelstan's mother, had to go. So too, effectively, did Athelstan. Eldest son of Edward though he was, his pedigree would be as nothing compared to that of such children as Ælfflæd might bear her husband – for their inheritance would be doubly royal. It was the mark of the significance placed by Edward on his new wife's bloodline that he chose to grace her with an honour that ran directly contrary to West Saxon custom: consecration. Ecgwynn, certainly, had never been anointed as a queen. The awesome spectacle of Ælfflæd being touched with holy oil could only rub home the contrast with her uncle Æthelwold, a renegade among the Viking heathen. It also emphasized the degree to which Athelstan faced being superseded. Sure enough, it did not take the new queen long to get pregnant. Her child, when she came to term, proved to be a boy. Ælfweard, as he was named by his parents, was immediately enshrined as his father's heir. Already, by 901, while still a tiny baby, he was being recorded as a witness to one of his father's charters. So too, it was true, was Athelstan; but his name was listed below that of his half-brother. His new place in the line of succession could hardly have been made any clearer. Perhaps, then, it was not surprising that his father should have decided to separate him from Ælfweard. The presence of Æthelwold among the Vikings of the North was a menacing reminder of just how bitter rivalries within the royal household might become if allowed to get out of hand. Wessex, in Edward's opinion, was too small for both his sons. Fortunately, though, it was not the only kingdom which acknowledged him as its lord.

It was back in 874 that the last independent king of Mercia had fled Britain. The Vikings, treating his abandoned kingdom as they had sought to treat Wessex, had appointed a puppet in his place, and then pointedly made winter camp at Repton, where the mausoleum of the Mercian royal family lay: a brutal desecration. Only with Alfred's great victory four years later had the yoke partially been lifted; for by the terms of the treaty agreed with the defeated pagans, Mercia had been divided into rival spheres of influence, Viking and West Saxon. Alfred, lacking sufficient support among the Mercian ealdormen to rule directly over the western half of the kingdom assigned to him, had known better than to push his luck. Old enemies though Wessex and Mercia were, the shared menace posed to their survival by the heathen invaders had long since persuaded them to set aside their traditional enmities. Alfred himself had been self-evidently fond of Mercians. His own wife, Ealhswith, was one, and so too was Plegmund, 'the estimable man richly endowed with learning'[5] whom in 890 he had appointed Archbishop of Canterbury. As a result, when Alfred laid claim to the overlordship of western Mercia, he was able to moderate the inevitable resentment of his new subjects by presenting himself as a ruler familiar with their customs and respectful of their traditions. The Mercians, by and large, had been content in return to offer him their loyalty: for they had recognized in the West Saxon king the one man capable of taking the fight to the heathen. In 893, during the course of the Viking invasion which had seen Edward secure his great victory at Farnham, a Mercian task force had provided him with reinforcements at a particularly key moment. Unsurprisingly, then, in Mercia as in Wessex, there were few who really doubted that the two kingdoms were better together.

As a result, when Edward scouted around for a court beyond the limits of Wessex where his eldest son might be brought up, he did not have far to look. Although the Mercians no longer had a king, they did now have a ruler whom the Welsh and the Irish, ignorant of the subtleties of politics among the 'Saxons', were prone to hailing as one. The ambivalence, perhaps, was deliberate. Æthelred, who had first emerged as the greatest man in Mercia in succession to the Vikings' puppet king, offered his people the reassurance that they were not merely West Saxon subjects. Graced with the title of '*subregulus*' in Alfred's charters – 'junior king' – he was known in Mercia itself as '*Myrcna Hlaford*': 'Lord of the Mercians'. Such a man, in Edward's opinion, was doubly qualified to raise his eldest son. Not only were the two of them old comrades in arms, veterans together of the defeat of the Vikings back in 893, but the lord of the Mercians also ranked as something more – as family. His wife was Edward's own elder sister, in whose veins there flowed Mercian as well as West Saxon blood: a woman of steely resolve and ability by the name of Æthelflæd.

'So it was provided that Athelstan should be educated at the court of Alfred's daughter, Æthelflæd, and of his son-in-law, Æthelred.'[6] This tradition, that the young *ætheling* had been sent to Mercia, there to be brought up by his aunt, was one that no surviving source from Athelstan's own lifetime explicitly confirms: but the fact that the Mercians, in time, would come to see him as one of their own, and prove deeply loyal to him as such, provides near-certain corroboration.[7] Like father, like daughter: Æthelflæd was devout, learned and no less martial in her ambitions for her adopted people than any man. The court of such a woman was to prove a fit training ground for her nephew. Alfred's influence on his daughter, his commitment to the arts of peace as well as to those of war, was one that she in turn would exert on Athelstan. Nobody was ever to cast aspersions on his aptitude for battle; but even as a young child he could be hailed as well for his devotion both to Christ and to scholarship. 'Abundantly are you endowed with the holy eminence of learning.'[8] Whatever else the effect on Athelstan of the humiliation of his mother, and of his own exile from his father's court, it did not impair his determination to prove himself worthy of his pedigree: to be an *ætheling* in more than name.

Meanwhile, on a vastly broader stage, a drama that had already convulsed the house of Wessex was approaching its sanguinary climax. In 901, Æthelwold appeared at the head of a great fleet in the Thames estuary. Essex, where he landed, marked a frontier zone between Edward's kingdom and the lands beyond it granted by treaty to the Vikings, and which later chroniclers would term the '*Dena lage*': the 'Danelaw'. Æthelwold, determined to reclaim his patrimony, did not hesitate to raise his banner in open warfare against his cousin. A year after his arrival in Essex, he crossed the frontier of the Danelaw, and invaded Mercia. With him rode a teeming and loot-hungry host: pagans from the North, warlords from the Danelaw itself and even, it may be, dispossessed members of the Mercian royal line.[9] As Edward frantically sought to raise forces to meet them, so Æthelwold was fording the Thames, ravaging the northern limits of Wessex, and then, laden down with plunder, heading back to East Anglia. Here it was, amid the marshes and flatness of the Fens, that Edward at last caught up with him. The carnage was terrible. Both Æthelwold and the King of the Danelaw, claimed by the sucking mud, 'were pulled down into the world below'.[10] No less, though, was the slaughter among the ranks of Edward's men. Ultimately, it was the Vikings who were left in possession of the battlefield; and in the bloody rearguard action which covered the West Saxon retreat, the ealdorman of Kent, Sigehelm, was a notable casualty. Naturally, with Æthelwold eliminated, Edward could still reckon his main objective successfully achieved – but it had been a close-run thing, even so.

Twice in ten years a Viking army had menaced the heartland of the West Saxon dynasty; and twice, thanks to his own tireless efforts, Edward had succeeded in stabilizing the frontiers of his kingdom. The experience confirmed him in a fateful conviction: that ultimately, faced by enemies as predatory and opportunistic as the Vikings, it was only by toppling their kings, and forcing them at sword-point to acknowledge his own overlordship, that Wessex would ever be able to enjoy true security. Such an ambition, self-evidently, was no easy one to meet. Edward, though, was a master of long-term planning. Schooled in his father's counsels and seasoned by a decade of campaigning, he well understood patience and careful preparation to be the necessary preconditions of any programme of conquest. Massive effort as well. *Burh*s, the fortified towns planted by Alfred along the limits of Wessex, had repeatedly stood firm against the lapping tides of Viking invasions; but Edward's aim was to deploy them for offensive as well as defensive purposes. The expense and manpower required to render such a strategy effective was bound, of course, to prove immense; but Edward was prepared to take his time. As token of this, on many of his coins he stamped a potent symbol: the barred gates of a *burh*. With perhaps a quarter of all Edward's adult male subjects involved in either constructing or garrisoning his great network of forts, the image served to remind them of what they were: a single people, united in heroic purpose.

It was not only Wessex which could increasingly boast a formidable screen of *burh*s. The borders of Mercia, where the coins were stamped with towers, were starting to bristle in a similar fashion. Although Æthelred, much older than his wife and in ailing health, was no longer as active as he had been in his prime, Æthelflæd was more than capable of emulating her brother's efforts. As Edward, in the decade that followed the death of Æthelhelm, sought to buttress his frontier with the Danelaw against any future pretender to his throne, so his sister, on the shores of the

Irish Sea, was preoccupied by an altogether more immediate threat. The sea lanes between Britain and Ireland were filling with dragon ships. In 902, the year of Æthelwold's death in the Fens, a sixty-year-old Viking stronghold beside the mouth of the River Liffey had been overwhelmed and its inhabitants expelled. The King of Dublin, as the settlement was called, had headed northwards for Alba, the realm ruled by Constantin, King of the Scots, and there, a couple of years later, been killed in battle. Others of the exiled Dubliners, though, had made a shorter journey. It was an easy crossing from the Liffey to the western seaboard of Northumbria. Æthelflæd, marking with alarm the growing numbers of Viking settlers on Mercia's northern doorstep, did what she could to regulate the immigration. Those coming to her with a request for lands, she settled on the Wirral; but at the same time, suspicious as only a daughter of Alfred could be of Viking opportunism, she looked around for means to keep them bottled up. Fortunately, just south of the peninsula, there stretched the dilapidated walls and weed-covered streets of a long-abandoned ghost town: the Roman city of Chester. Already, back in 892, a fugitive warband of Vikings had briefly camped out amid its ruins; and Æthelflæd, fifteen years on, was determined not to let it fall a second time into enemy hands. Accordingly, in 907 she renovated the city. Walls were patched up, gates repaired, a garrison installed. The transformation of Chester into Mercia's northernmost *burh* was completed just in time. When the Viking settlers on the Wirral, tiring of the lands they had been given, and looking around for fresh pickings, sought to seize the city, their attack was rebuffed. Tales of the siege, improved with every retelling, would end up the toast of Ireland: how the defenders had poured boiling beer over their assailants, and then 'let loose on the attacking force all the beehives in the town, so that they could not move their legs or hands from the great number of bees stinging them'.[11]

Æthelflæd attracted such stories. Shield of her people, she wore about her the palpable aura of queens from ancient song. In 909, when Edward, in a significant escalation of his preparations for pacifying the Danelaw, led an army of West Saxons and Mercians into eastern Mercia and ravaged it for over a month, his sister's contribution to the campaign was an exploit of numinous boldness. 'In this year, the body of Saint Oswald was brought from Bardney into Mercia.'[12] Escorted in triumph from the depths of Viking-held territory, the relics were laid to rest in Gloucester: a favourite place of Æthelflæd and her husband. Like Chester, it had originally been a wasteland of weeds and Roman ruins, the haunt of heathen warbands, before its redemption by their workmen. Now, entrusting the remains of Saint Oswald to a church they had founded in the town, she endowed it, and her own dynasty, with the potency of the dead king's charisma. At Chester, the relics of a Mercian saint had been placed within a church, there to touch the *burh*'s defences with the charge of his holiness; but the presence in Gloucester of Northumbria's most celebrated warrior saint, as formidable in battle as he had been renowned for his love of Christ, served to illumine the whole of Mercia with an awesome radiance.

Æthelflæd too was similarly graced. Her feat had placed her in an epic light: as a woman worthy of comparison with those who, back in the heroic age of Saint Oswald, had first sought to banish the worship of Woden from the feasting halls and forests of Britain. Sure confirmation of this was to come the following year. A great army of Vikings, laden down with plunder and returning from a sweep through Æthelflæd's lands that had taken them as far as Wessex, were ambushed at a river crossing near Tettenhall and wiped out in a storm of spears. Three of their kings fell in the slaughter, 'hastening to the hall of the Infernal One'.[13] An entire generation of their warriors was maimed. Infallible token of God's hand was to be found in the site of the great battle, for it preserved in its name the echo of earlier, darker times, before the light of Christ had purged the shadows: Woden's Field.

The lessons taught Athelstan by his aunt's campaigning style were to prove enduring ones. A readiness to commit to the bold action; an eye for an adversary's weakness; a deep faith in the tutelary power of relics: here were examples of behaviour which could hardly help but have a strong influence on the young *ætheling*. Solemnly he vowed to Æthelred that he would always keep the church built to house Saint Oswald in his favour: 'a pact of paternal piety'.[14] Yet even as he was making this pledge to his foster-father, there remained no assurance that he would ever be in a position to fulfil it. In 911, after a long illness, Æthelred died; and Edward, moving quickly, annexed the Thames valley as far as Oxford directly to his rule. Beyond that, though, he did not go; and Æthelflæd, the sister who had always so loyally served his interests, remained in Mercia as its ruler. In succession to her husband, she was now acknowledged by her subjects as '*Myrcna Hlæfdige*', 'the Lady of the Mercians'; but in the reaches beyond her kingdom, where her name was spoken in awed terms, she had come to be hailed as 'the ever renowned Queen of the Saxons'.[15] Such ambivalence rendered her a fit guardian for her nephew. Athelstan's own status remained ambiguous as well. Back in Wessex, Ælfflæd had continued to provide Edward with a steady succession of children: a second son, Edwin, and some five or six daughters. Just as Athelstan could command the loyalty of the Mercians, so Ælfweard, Ælfflæd's eldest son, had been raised in Wessex, amid the ealdormen and levies of the West Saxons. Which of the two *ætheling*s, if either, would succeed to their father as '*rex Angul-Saxonum*' – 'king of the Anglo-Saxons' – remained an open question. Indeed, lurking behind it remained a very different possibility: that Mercia and Wessex might end up divided between the rival princes, and the two kingdoms once again go their separate ways. The future of Edward's realm remained far from clear.

Yet one thing, over the course of the decade that followed the great victory at Woden's Field, was to become perfectly evident: that the combined resources of Wessex and Mercia, when harnessed by leaders of rare ability, more than had the beating of the Danelaw. With Edward and Æthelflæd both still tireless in their construction of *burh*s, the first co-ordinated infrastructure project of the nascent Anglo-Saxon kingdom was, by 916, nearing completion. A great line of fortresses had come to run the whole way from Essex to the Mersey. The moment long prepared for by Edward was finally at hand. With Wessex and Mercia both impregnably defended, he had won for himself the opportunity to crush the Danelaw once and for all. It was his foes themselves who delivered it up to him. When, in the spring of 917, Edward made a brutal statement of intent by planting yet another *burh* deep within enemy territory and seizing one of the Vikings' own fortresses, the attempt by his adversaries to roll back his advancing line of fortifications dissolved into a series of razzias so aimless and undisciplined as to leave their western flank perilously exposed. That summer, when Æthelflæd rode out from behind her line of *burh*s into Viking-held Mercia, there was no one to stop her. Derby, long a stronghold of her adversaries' power, fell easily into her hands. Further triumphs then followed in quick succession. The King of the Danelaw was killed when the fortress he had holed himself up in was stormed. Colchester was captured and its population put to the sword. The *jarl* of Northampton and his men, rather than meet Edward in the field, surrendered to him, 'and sought to have him as their protector and lord'. By Christmas, all the Vikings of East Anglia had been brought to do the same, swearing that 'they would do everything as he commanded them to do'.[16] The unforced submission early in the new year of Leicester to Æthelflæd brought home the full startling transformation that the previous twelve months had witnessed: the effective subordination of everywhere south of the Humber to the lordship of the West Saxon king.

Yet at the very moment of his triumph, Edward was obliged to pause in his campaign. On 12 June he suffered a grievous loss: the great partner of his efforts, 'comfort of his subjects, and terror of his foes'.[17] Fittingly, the Lady of the Mercians died in Tamworth, the stronghold which once, before its sack by the Vikings, had been the capital of an independent Mercia, and the seat of its greatest kings. Æthelflæd herself had restored it, patching up its fortifications and favouring it as her principal residence; but Edward, sweeping into the town upon the news of his sister's death, had no intention of pandering to its pretensions. Ordering the removal of Æthelflæd's body to Gloucester, to be buried alongside her husband and the relics of Saint Oswald, he obliged the Mercian ealdormen formally to submit to him as their king. Only the continued presence in Mercia of Æthelflæd's one child, a daughter by the name of Ælfwynn, gave them hope that they might at some point be ruled again by a Lady of the Mercians; but in 919 even that fig-leaf of independence was ripped away from them when Edward had his niece packed off south of the border. Wessex and Mercia, joined now unambiguously under the single king, appeared transfigured into a single, united kingdom.

But for how long? Even Edward himself seemed to fear the possibility of overstretch: that by annexing so much territory, and in such a fell swoop, he risked becoming the victim of his own ambitions. His solution, as it had been when facing down a challenge once before, was to take a new wife. Ælfflæd, treated much as Athelstan's mother had earlier been, was packed off to a nunnery, and replaced in the royal marriage bed by a woman more immediately suited to his purposes. Eadgifu was the daughter of Sige-helm, the heroic ealdorman of Kent whose rearguard action back in 903 had helped the West Saxons to with-draw from the Fens. By marrying her, and then fathering on her two sons, Edmund and Eadred, in quick succession, Edward could rest confident that he had cemented the loy-alty of his Kentish subjects. This, at a time when he was increasingly absent on the northern limits of Mercia, was a vital reassurance. He could not afford distractions. There were the last remaining pockets of Viking resistance south of the Humber to mop up, and Mercian loyalties to secure. On both counts, the long residence of Athelstan at his aunt's court had helped to render him a key asset. While Ælfweard, Edward's eldest son by Ælfflæd, remained in the heartlands of the kingdom in Wessex, Athelstan seems to have been kept busy by his father's side in the northern marches of Mercia. Such, at any rate, is the implication of events in the summer of 924 when, at a ford just south of Chester, death at last caught up with the *rex Angul-Saxonum*. The Mercians, without more ado, hailed Athelstan as their king. If he was not directly by Edward's side as he breathed his last, the *ætheling* was clearly in the immediate vicinity. This was what gave him his head start. Meanwhile, bearing news of the great king's death, a horseman was galloping southwards, bound for Wessex, and Ælfweard.

Few doubted that the future of the Anglo-Saxon realm carved out over the course of Edward's long and epochal reign had been left hanging in the balance. No matter how remarkable his feats, the prospect of his kingdom fracturing now that he was dead had to be reckoned very real. Nor was it only the West Saxons and Mercians who awaited events with bated breath. Despite all Edward's efforts, the frontiers of his kingdom remained far from secure. Centuries later, tales would be told of the troubled circumstances that had preceded his death: of a rebellion crushed in Chester, and incursions by the Welsh.[18] True or not, they certainly corresponded to the turbulent reality of the circumstances faced by Athelstan. As his father had done on the death of Alfred, he faced grievous challenges: enemies on his borders and dynastic tensions in his heartlands. Many kingdoms had risen to primacy before in Britain, only to crumble away. It was now on Athelstan's shoulders to ensure that the realm forged by his grandfather and father did not follow a similar path. South of the Humber and north, men watched and waited, to see what Athelstan would make of the great challenges bequeathed him by Edward – and of the no less dazzling opportunities.

3
Northumbria

In Wessex, the news of Edward's death and of the election
by the Mercians of Athelstan as their king was greeted by
many with dismay. This was particularly so in the *burh*
which over the course of the previous decades had come to
rank as the undoubted heart of the kingdom: Winchester.
Nowhere spoke more splendidly of the dignity of the house
of Wessex. A great double ditch surrounded renovated
Roman walls; but within their circuit, only the central
high street remained of the town's ancient layout. Æthelflæd, when she rebuilt Chester and Gloucester, had been
following her father's example: for Alfred, resolved to
fashion Winchester into a capital commensurate with
his ambitions for Wessex, had laid out almost six miles of
cobbled roads. Channels ran alongside each new street, to
supply drinking water to the burgeoning population and to
power the city's mills; market stalls crowded the high
street selling gold and silverware, swords and shoes; tene-
ments jostled for space with churches. The most impressive
development of all lay in the south-eastern quarter of the
city, where both the royal court and the venerable seat of
Winchester's bishop, the minster, were to be found. Alfred,
never the man to let slip a chance to improve on his

inheritance, had commissioned an entire new minster, and
Ealhswith, his wife, a nunnery. These two developments
had finally been completed under their son; and Edward,
once the New Minster was ready to receive his parents'
mortal remains, had solemnly had them reinterred. Now,
upon the tidings brought from Mercia, preparations began
to be made to receive Edward's own body – for no one
doubted that he too would be laid to rest in the New Minster. A king of Wessex, it had come to be expected, should
always end up in Winchester.

Except that Athelstan, the man proclaimed king by the
Mercians, had spent more than two decades in exile from
the city. Now almost thirty, he had grown up a stranger to
its court. Unsurprisingly, then, there were plenty in Winchester who were inclined to look on him almost as a
pretender. Their loyalty instead was to Ælfweard. Better
an *ætheling* who had grown up in the West Saxon court,
and could be relied upon to defend its interests – even
though he was some five years Athelstan's junior – than
one who ranked in their eyes virtually as a Mercian.
Unsurprisingly, then, with memories still vivid of the crisis
that had afflicted Wessex upon the previous death of a
king, rumours in Winchester were rife. Ælfweard, rather
than await the arrival of his father's mortal remains in the
New Minster, was reported to be directly on the West
Saxon frontier with Mercia, in Oxford. Then, barely a
fortnight after the arrival in Winchester of the news
of Edward's death, came even more shocking tidings:
Ælfweard too was dead. The circumstances, no matter
how convenient for Athelstan, were not alleged to be

suspicious. Certainly, no story to that effect ever gained wide currency. Athelstan, seasoned both in warfare and statecraft, moved quickly to press his claim to the kingship of Wessex, and to ensure that his younger half-brother, Edwin, was never seriously spoken of as a contender for their father's throne. Nevertheless, in Winchester there was grumbling and discontent. The city's bishop ostentatiously refused to witness Athelstan's charters. Scribes working in the New Minster omitted his name completely from their list of West Saxon kings. Centuries later, stories were still being repeated of the plots and counter-plots that had swirled through the royal court in the wake of Ælfweard's death: of a conspiracy to seize Athelstan and put out his eyes, and of how the conspirators, 'on the discovery of their infernal contrivances, had been sent to defend themselves before the Pope in Rome'.[1]

True or not, it was the measure of the opposition faced by Athelstan in Wessex that a whole year passed before the new king at last felt secure enough to stage his consecration – and that when he did so, it was not in Winchester. Instead, on 4 September 925, ealdormen and bishops alike assembled in Surrey, at Kingston. The message conveyed by this choice of location could hardly have been any clearer: for the Thames, the great river on which the '*Cyninges tun*' – the 'royal estate' – stood, had long served as the frontier between Wessex and Mercia. This was why, back in 886, when 'all the English people that were not under subjection to the Danes'[2] had formally acknowledged Alfred as their overlord, the ceremony had been held downriver from Kingston, in London; and it was why, in token of his determination to rule as more than just a king of Wessex, he had made a point of renovating the long-abandoned Roman capital, and enshrining it as a city that could rank as authentically Anglo-Saxon. By the time of Athelstan's consecration, the Thames estuary, no longer churned by the oars of Viking dragon ships, had become a scene of prosperity and peace. Boats crammed the wharfs built by Alfred within the ancient walls of London; fields stretched unburnt down to the banks of the river as it snaked inland; Kingston, set amid the colours of ripening harvest, provided a fit stage for the awesome ritual about to unfold.

Never before in Britain had there been a consecration quite like it. Æthelhelm, the successor to Plegmund as Archbishop of Canterbury, had prepared for it with great care.[3] It was the aim of the liturgy that he had specially composed for the occasion to set the seal on the union of Wessex and Mercia. Athelstan, so the archbishop repeatedly reminded his congregation, had been elected as king of both realms '*pariter*' – 'equally'. Invited to acclaim their new lord, West Saxon ealdormen and Mercian did so resoundingly as one. Then, after urging Athelstan to emulate the example of David, just as his grandfather had done, Æthelhelm anointed him with holy oil. It was not just to the Bible, though, that the king and his archbishop looked for their inspiration. Of the various tokens of royal authority presented to Athelstan at the ceremony – a ring, a sword, a sceptre – none was quite so telling as the one lowered by Æthelhelm onto his head. Primordial tradition decreed that this be a helmet; but Athelstan had opted instead for an emblem that was altogether more imperial. The emperors of Rome, whose sway back in ancient times had been of an almost unimaginable order, could be seen on their coins, when these were dug up from the earth, wearing a variety of circlets: some fashioned out of leaves, others of gold and jewels, others yet adorned with spikes, like the rays of the sun. In AD 800 Charlemagne, the son of Pepin, had been crowned in Rome by the pope himself, and the sprawling array of his territories, which stretched from Saxony to the Pyrenees, proclaimed a reborn Roman Empire. Even though, over the course of the century that followed, the dominion of the Franks – 'Francia', as it was called – had progressively splintered, its various kings still sported jewel-encrusted circlets as the definitive emblem of their rank. Now, with the lowering onto Athelstan's head of a crown, a touch of Rome had been brought to the banks of the Thames. Consecration had been rendered a coronation.

Strikingly, however, Athelstan had no one beside him as he was crowned. Even though Edward, with his marriage to Ælfflæd, had legitimized the notion that the wife of a West Saxon king might be consecrated, there was no new queen anointed in Kingston. Athelstan had never married – nor would he. This, for a man of royal blood, let alone a king, was sufficiently unusual to provoke the raising of the odd eyebrow. The propagation of heirs, as Edward had so fecundly demonstrated, was a responsibility that few kings opted to shirk. Yet Athelstan, whose own childhood had been shaken by a bloody contest between rival cousins, and who had only succeeded to the entirety of his father's lands by virtue of his brother's fortuitously timed death, had good cause to reflect on the troubles that a king might breed by fathering sons. Certainly, with three half-brothers at his court, he suffered from no immediate lack of heirs. What deals might conceivably have been struck before his coronation, what negotiations settled, what promises given, was not openly bruited. Nevertheless, the implications of Athelstan's celibacy for the long-term prospects of his realm were self-evident. There would be no *æthelings* bred of the reigning king to challenge his brothers. Athelstan, putting the interests of his still rickety kingdom above the promptings of his own carnal nature, had doubly consecrated himself to the service of his people.[4] *Rex pius* indeed.

Yet it was not sufficient merely to bind the fractures that had threatened the union between Wessex and Mercia, and the coherence of his own dynasty. Athelstan, like his father and his grandfather before him, faced mortal enemies beyond the limits of his kingdom. The conquest of the Danelaw south of the Humber had not eliminated the Viking menace. York, an ancient foundation that could boast a mighty circuit of Roman walls, the seat of an archbishop, and teeming markets piled with everything from Swedish amber to Byzantine silks, had for half a century been a formidable stronghold of the heathen. Hewn out of the carcass of Northumbria, the agglomeration of lands ruled from the city was both the most enduring and the most formidable Viking kingdom in Britain. Its rulers had put down deep roots. The violence of their initial conquest of Northumbria, which had seen Christian kings despatched in brutal fashion and churches stripped bare, had been moderated over the years by a recognition that the faith of the conquered might after all have its uses. The Archbishop of York, whose influence over his flock was of an order sufficient to impress even pagan warlords, had offered particularly productive collaboration. One Viking king of the city had ended up buried in the minster. Another had issued coins with his name laid out in the form of a cross. Athelstan, looking to the North and wondering how best to secure his borders, could recognize in the kingdom of York powerful elements that ranked as Christian.

Yet a Viking realm it remained, nevertheless. The original conquerors of the city, who in 905 had found themselves unable even to agree on a king, had fallen into eclipse. In their place a new regime had come to power. Edward and Æthelflæd were not the only siblings to have devoted themselves in the decade before Athelstan's accession to expanding their sway. Ragnald and Sihtric, two grandsons of the warlord who had founded the kingdom of Dublin, had refused to accept the loss of their family's Irish stronghold as a terminal block on their ambitions. A decade after being driven from Ireland, their comeback had begun to take shape. In 914 Ragnald had won a great victory in the waters off the Isle of Man; three years later his brother had returned in triumph to Dublin as its king; in 919 Ragnald himself had attacked and captured York. Buccaneering, restless and aggressively pagan, he had appeared to his followers a warlord sprung from the golden age of Viking empire-building. He seemed so to his enemies as well. With York in Ragnald's hands, and Sihtric installed in Dublin, the dominion forged by the two brothers had come to span the Irish Sea: a feat of conquest fit to compare with that of Edward himself.

No wonder, then, in the final years of his reign, that Athelstan's father should have been much preoccupied with events in York. Ragnald's capture of the city had served as a sobering reminder that the Viking menace, diminished though it certainly was, remained hydra-like. Nevertheless, when Edward succeeded to his sister's direct rule of Mercia, it had been to a skilfully constructed policy of containment as well. Æthelflæd, alert to the danger posed by Viking adventurers as only a daughter of Alfred could be, had built a line of fortresses along the Mersey, blocking the readiest line of communication between York and Dublin; she had forged alliances with the kings of Alba and Strathclyde, both of whom had suffered maulings from Ragnald, and dreaded his ambitions; she had even won the backing of collaborators within York itself. True, none of these initiatives had been sufficient to prevent Ragnald, the year after Æthelflæd's death, from capturing the city; but they had provided Edward with an invaluable basis from which to respond to the crisis. In an aggressive statement of intent, he had advanced into Viking-held territory, and for the first time occupied and refortified an abandoned Roman fortress directly in Northumbria: Manchester. Then, in 920, he had taken full advantage of the great web of alliances woven by his sister, and invited leaders from across the North to an unprecedented pan-British summit.[5] Constantin of Alba, Owain, the King of Strathclyde, and a host of other lords from across Northumbria – English and Scandinavian both – had travelled to meet with Edward. That so many should have answered the summons of the Anglo-Saxon king was as potent a demonstration of his primacy within Britain as could possibly have been staged; and it was no surprise that his propagandists should have made much of it. 'All who came chose him as father and lord.'[6] An exaggeration, no doubt; but due reflection, indisputably, of Edward's ability to fashion and impose a peace accord. Surest proof of this had been the presence at the summit of none other than the thunderbolt of the North: Ragnald himself. Marking the array of kings gathering at Edward's side, he had evidently decided that the time was ripe to bank his winnings. Peace with his neighbours in exchange for recognition of his right to the kingdom of York: such essentially had been the deal. It was one which Athelstan, now that he had succeeded to Edward's throne, had to decide whether to reaffirm.

His initial policy, as his father's had been, was twofold: to maintain a strong military presence in the northern marches of his kingdom, while simultaneously talking the language of peace. In this, Athelstan was much helped by his possession of a large reserve of diplomatic counters: some eight or nine sisters. Marriage negotiations were duly opened to secure a union between his own house and that of the upstart King of York. Naturally, it was out of the question for a Christian princess, and a granddaughter of Alfred at that, to marry a worshipper of idols: a consideration that might have presented an insuperable problem had the inveterately pagan Ragnald still been alive. He had died, though, back in 921; and Sihtric, who had crossed from Dublin to take possession of York in his brother's place, proved himself amenable to Athelstan's conditions. He accepted baptism. Then, early in 926, he crossed into Mercia to claim his prize. There, on 30 January, the marriage was celebrated in Tamworth, the ancient capital lately restored by Athelstan's aunt, and a fitting venue for what appeared a decisive moment in the history of Britain. Relations between the two greatest kings in the island, Anglo-Saxon and Viking, had at last been set on a stable footing.

Or so it seemed. Within a year, though, blazing in the northern sky, fiery lights were serving as the portents of an utter convulsion in the affairs of Britain – one that would leave the contours of its various realms momentously altered. In 927, Sihtric died. At once, messengers set out from York to Dublin. There, ruling as Sihtric's deputy, was his cousin, Guthfrith. He was the obvious heir. Just as Sihtric had succeeded Ragnald, so now, it was assumed by their followers, would Guthfrith succeed Sihtric. Yet the distance between York and Dublin was much greater than that between the city and the frontier with Athelstan's kingdom. The Anglo-Saxon king, brought the news of Sihtric's death, did not hesitate. The opportunity presented by the interregnum in York was too good for a man of Athelstan's daring and decisiveness to miss. Orders were given; the fortresses built by Æthelflæd and Edward along the northern marches emptied of their troops; the border crossed. When Athelstan appeared before the walls of

York, there was no one to resist him. Guthfrith, crossing the Irish Sea to claim his inheritance, found that it had slipped through his fingers. Already, with the capital of the North in his hands, York's new master was moving to stamp it as his own. Gold and silver plundered from Sihtric's treasury were distributed among his followers; strongholds of Viking power within the city walls pulled down. Coins minted in the city on Athelstan's orders bore a momentous slogan: *'rex Anglorum'*.

Admittedly, this was not the first time that the phrase had been used to describe him. Back in the troubled early months of his reign, prior to his coronation, when many in Wessex were still withholding their loyalty, it had appeared in a charter witnessed solely by Mercians, to specify that he was the king of an Anglian, not a Saxon, realm: 'by indulgence of divine clemency King of the Angles'.[7] The implications of the slogan now that Athelstan had conquered York, however, were very different. Even though his overwhelming objective in seizing the city had been to eliminate the last Viking kingdom in Britain, he was not oblivious to the additional prize that his feat had won him. Once, in its heyday, the Anglian kingdom of Northumbria had extended from the Humber to the Firth of Forth, and Athelstan, despite the fact that Ragnald's writ had been more circumscribed, saw no reason why his should be. *Rex Anglorum*: all the Angles of Britain, from Lothian to the Thames, were henceforward to acknowledge the single king. Yet Athelstan's purpose in deploying the phrase was more ambitious still. Bede, in his great history of the coming of the Christian faith to Britain, had described how the future Pope Gregory, walking through Rome's slave market, had marvelled at the beauty of the Northumbrian boys he saw there, and proclaimed them to be not Angles but 'angeli' – 'angels'. A fateful pun. Alfred, whose respect for Gregory was such that he had personally translated the pope's meditation on the qualities required of a ruler, had certainly been alert to its implications. It had prompted him, in his attempt to find a word that might describe both his West Saxon and his Mercian subjects, to settle on 'Angelcynn' – 'English'. Implicit in his promotion of the term had been a sense that all those who shared with him the same language constituted a single people: for it was God Himself, by whose providence Gregory had come to see boys from Northumbria in Rome's slave market, who conceived of them as such. Whether of Wessex, of Mercia or of Northumbria, all were to be ranked as English.

Nevertheless, lurking behind this vision, of an agglomeration of kingdoms that might plausibly be termed 'Englalonde', there was to be found an infinitely more ancient ideal: that of an empire spanning the whole of Britain. Settled though it was by 'peoples divided by language and separated by race according to their ancestors' names',[8] yet the dream of establishing a pan-British order was one that many of them shared. In Wales, poets foretold a time when the whole island would once again be theirs; in the Highlands, the Scots pointedly termed their kingdom 'Alba', the venerable Gaelic word for 'Britain'; in Canterbury, the archbishop regarded himself as Primate of the entire British Church. It was hardly to be expected, then, that Athelstan, in the wake of his conquest of York, would rest content with laying claim merely to the rule of the English.

Sure enough, in the summer of the fateful year of 927 he convened a meeting that made explicit his determination to serve as *'rex totius Britanniae'* – 'the king of the whole of Britain'. Crossing the Pennines, he made for Penrith, and the southernmost limits of the kingdom of Strathclyde. Savage though the landscape was, an untamed wilderness of mountains and lakes, yet Athelstan had chosen the location for his summit well. Welsh-speaking Cumbrians, English-speaking Northumbrians, Norse-speaking Scandinavians: all were to be found there. So too were ghosts. Halting beside the River Eamont, Athelstan fixed his camp in the shadow of monuments which, fashioned in ancient times, bore witness to others whose sway had been of an imperial scope: standing stones and great banks of turf raised by the giants who had originally inhabited the island, and a fortress built by the Romans. The message conveyed to the kings and lords summoned from across Britain, from Alba, and Lothian, and Wales, was an intimidating one. Less than a decade had passed since their meeting with Edward on the northern frontier of Mercia, but in that space of time everything had changed. There could be no veiling now what was being demanded of them: acknowledgement of Athelstan's lordship. Sure enough, on 12 July, 'all the kings of the island were brought under his rule'. Submission was made; payments of tribute pledged; oaths sworn that no dealings would ever again be had with the heathen Vikings. 'And afterwards all departed in peace.'[9]

Among them, heading south, was Athelstan himself. Despite the scale and the sweep of his conquests, he knew better than to put too much trust in his own propaganda. He was not fooled by his own claim to the mastery of Britain into thinking that he could take the loyalty of his heartlands for granted. With a fractious capital, a dispossessed half-brother in the form of Edwin and memories of his troubled accession still fresh, Athelstan had no wish to linger in the North longer than was necessary. Pausing on his journey southwards only to receive the taxes of various Welsh princes, and their public acknowledgement of him as a '*Mechteyrn*'[10] – a 'Great King' – he continued to his ancestral realm. Here, for the next seven years, he would largely remain, travelling tirelessly from *burh* to *burh* and estate to estate. Yet though in this he was as much a king of Wessex as his forefathers had ever been, his gaze remained firmly set on the limits of Britain. Athelstan was not the man to treat oaths of submission to him lightly. 'Guard against the anger of God and insubordination to me.'[11]

There was no one so great who, having accepted him as lord, would not be expected to obey a call to his court. The Primates of both Canterbury and York; kings from Wales; *jarls* from the Danelaw; ealdormen and bishops from every corner of his kingdom: all were now obliged to head for Wessex when the summons from Athelstan went out. Never before in Britain had there been a royal council which comprised so many different people from so many different corners of the island. Scribes keeping record of its dealings, of the lands bestowed, the laws enacted and the tributes demanded by their king, fashioned ever more splendid sobriquets in their effort to keep pace with his greatness. Who could doubt, witnessing him surrounded by upwards of a hundred princes, bishops and lords, that he was indeed what his charters proclaimed him to be: 'raised by the right hand of God Almighty to the throne of the entire kingdom of Britain'?[12]

Nevertheless, despite the conquest of York and the oaths sworn on the banks of the Eamont, there remained limits to what even the potency of Athelstan could command. Neither Owain, the King of the Cumbrians, nor Constantin, the King of the Scots, deigned to come to his councils. The effort required to tame them, though, and to force their attendance appeared to carry too many risks. The road from Wessex to the banks of the Clyde was many hundreds of miles, and to Alba even longer. Nor had the considerations weighing on Athelstan's mind back in 927 entirely gone away. From Dublin, Guthfrith continued to eye the prize stolen from him by the English king, and to hanker after any opening that might enable him to seize it back. Meanwhile, in Wessex itself, subterranean rumours of conspiracy persisted. Although the Bishop of Winchester, a notable absentee from Athelstan's coronation, had made sure to join the king on his triumphant return from Eamont, the capital remained sullen. Edwin, whose blood was doubly royal, continued to provide an obvious focus for malcontents. The example of Æthelwold, the rebellious *ætheling* who had fled to the Vikings of York, served Athelstan as a salutary reminder of how the two biggest potential threats to his security might conceivably end up combining.

Yet circumstances, of course, could always change – and Athelstan had ever had an eye for opportunity. In 933, Edwin was drowned off the coast of Flanders. What he might have been doing out on the Channel was the subject of various rumours. A monk in the Flemish abbey where his corpse was interred recorded enigmatically that he had been driven from Wessex 'by some disturbance in the kingdom'.[13] Whatever the truth of this claim, Edwin's death certainly consolidated Athelstan's hold on power. His heir was now a twelve-year-old child: Edmund, the son of Edward by his third wife, Eadgifu. Such a boy, in the event of any expedition north, could be relied upon not to cause trouble. Then, the year after Edwin's shipwreck, the death was reported from Dublin of Guthfrith, and the succession to his throne by Olaf, his relatively untested son. Seven years previously, it was an interregnum in York that had given Athelstan his chance to mount an invasion of Northumbria. Now, with the death of Guthfrith, he sensed a similar opportunity. Once again, as he had done in 927, he would head north. On this occasion, though, his aim was to strike even further. Disloyalty was disloyalty, after all, no matter how far distant the culprit might be from Wessex. The time had come to teach this lesson to the most powerful of all the kings who had sworn submission to him at Eamont: Constantin of Alba.

In 934, Athelstan celebrated Pentecost at Winchester. A glittering occasion, at which the attendance of kings from Wales and *jarls* from the Danelaw was more than usually impressive, it was also an intimidating statement of intent. When Athelstan rode to war, he would do so not merely as

the *rex Anglorum*, but as 'king of the whole of Britain'.[14]
Punitive though his expedition against the Scots was certainly designed to be, it was something more as well: a
demonstration of his right to set the island in order. Riding
out with his army in late May, and then advancing at great
speed along the ancient road that led to the Roman Wall,
he made sure, even so, that his business was not entirely
that of war. When Athelstan, pausing at Nottingham,
granted lands between the Pennines and the Irish Sea to
Wulfstan, the Archbishop of York, it served as a reminder
to potential rebels that he had the power to reward as well
as to punish. Favours and the threat of force: such, as they
had ever been, were the essence of successful kingship. So
it was, after Athelstan's warriors had marched deep into
the Highlands, burning and looting as they went, and after
a fleet of his ships had ravaged the Scottish coastline the
whole way north to Caithness, that fresh terms were
offered to the King of Alba. Constantin, chastened by the
lethal display of force unleashed against his realm, had
little alternative but to accept them. That autumn, when
Athelstan returned to Wessex, no surer mark of his triumph was to be seen than the presence in his train of the
King of the Scots.

The ultimate display of his greatness, though, was
staged the following year. In 935, Athelstan sat in council
at Cirencester. Once, back in the distant past, Mercians
and West Saxons had fought a celebrated battle there, and
only sixty years before, during the reign of Alfred, Viking
warbands had made it their base. The times, though, had
healed. Just a short distance from Gloucester, where

Æthelflæd lay buried, Cirencester served as a monument to everything that she and her brother between them had forged: buttressed with walls, rich with markets, endowed with stone churches and towers. Fit theatre, then, for a celebration of their dynasty's remarkable achievement: the fashioning, over the course of only three generations, of a united kingdom that had come to span the whole of Britain. As witnesses to it, attendant in the royal council, were Constantin, and Owain, the King of Strathclyde, and the three most powerful princes of Wales. No one could doubt, seeing Athelstan enthroned amid the Roman relics of Cirencester, and crowned with a golden band radiate with spikes like the beams of the sun, that he deserved to be hailed as the emperor in far-off Constantinople was hailed: '*Basileus*'. He had proven himself, as even those beyond the Channel might acknowledge, a man of quite remarkable accomplishment: 'greatest and most illustrious of the kings who in our own day rule here on earth'.[15]

4
Angelcynn

One year before the great durbar at Cirencester, while leading his army northwards against the King of the Scots, Athelstan arrived beside the River Wear. Here he halted his army and made a brief diversion. His destination was a wooden church built some fifty years previously amid the ruins of an old Roman fort. Athelstan's enthusiasm for visiting Chester-le-Street was hardly surprising, for this small settlement contained treasures that richly merited a king's attention. The monks who escorted their royal guest into the church led him to a coffin. Then, as he watched, they removed the lid, so that its contents were revealed to his view. Inside the coffin lay the head of Oswald. It was, for the nephew of Æthelflæd, who had redeemed the saint's other mortal remains from the possession of the heathen, and brought them to Gloucester, an awe-inspiring thing to behold. There was, though, reverently laid beside it, an even more remarkable sight: a body wrapped in sumptuous silks and jewels, as incorrupt as on the very day that breath had left it. Nothing else in Britain could rival this corpse for sheer supernatural potency. Its holiness was manifest: a comfort to the faithful, a terror to the pagan. No wonder, then, that a king as renowned for his piety as

Athelstan should have paused in his expedition and come to pay his respects to Saint Cuthbert.

The bond between the house of Wessex and the most celebrated ascetic in Northumbria's history was a natural one. Both shared the same foe. Lindisfarne, the small island just north of Bamburgh where Cuthbert had originally been buried, had been pillaged by the Vikings as far back as 793: the very first monastery in Britain to be 'ravaged by heathen savages'.[1] By 875, with the Christian kingdom of Northumbria in ruins, the monks of the priory had despaired of their exposed location. Disinterring the body of their saintly patron, they had fled the island. An attempt to cross to Ireland had been halted when the Almighty battered their ship with waves of blood. Only in 883 had they finally settled at Chester-le-Street. Here, Cuthbert had shown himself more than capable of defending his own. Those who failed to treat him with due respect were struck with madness and a loathsome stench. Others, though, might be marked out by his favour to no less effect. Not long after his reburial, the saint had ordered an abbot to go to the Viking camp, and proclaim as king 'the slave of a certain widow';[2] and after the Vikings, miraculously swayed by this command, had done so, the new king had displayed his gratitude by granting Cuthbert a great swathe of lands south of the Tyne. Even the most inveterate of the pagans in York had known better than to risk the saint's anger by attempting to steal it back – until, that was, Ragnald had come to power. Appropriating Cuthbert's patrimony, he had divided it between two of his followers: 'sons of the Devil' both.[3] Sure enough, when one of them publicly insulted the saint, the wretch had promptly dropped down dead, and been claimed by the jaws of hell. 'St Cuthbert, as was just, regained his land.'[4] Yet it was only to be expected that the monks of Chester-le-Street, looking for an earthly as well as a heavenly patron, should have welcomed the coming to power in Northumbria of a Christian king. One could never have too many protectors, after all. Athelstan, devout and martial, seemed the answer to the church's prayers.

And the church the answer to his. Riding to war against the King of the Scots, Athelstan was under no illusions as to the precarious nature of his power in the North. To own as a loyal ally the principal power between the Tees and the Tyne appeared literally a godsend. For a king born in far-off Wessex, the favour of Northumbria's most loved and respected saint was a precious thing. This bond between the house of Cerdic and Cuthbert, so the monks who tended his shrine were pleased to report, was nothing new. In 878, at the lowest moment in Alfred's life, after he had been sent fleeing into the marshes of Somerset by the Viking ambush on Chippenham, the fugitive king had shared some of his scanty provisions with a passing stranger; and then, out on the waters, his men had hauled in a miraculous catch of fish. That same night, as Alfred lay in bed, the man to whom he had given hospitality had appeared in a vision, and revealed himself to be Cuthbert. The saint had promised Alfred victory over the Vikings, and that his descendants would rule the whole of Britain.[5] 'Be faithful to me and to my people, then, for all Albion has been given to you and your sons.'[6] To Athelstan the resonance of such a message was, of course, apparent.

His united kingdom of England was not merely sword-won, but blessed by Northumbria's most powerful saint.

It was not, though, mere dynastic considerations that had brought Athelstan to Cuthbert's shrine. Just as Æthelflæd, fortifying Chester or Gloucester, had known that the surest way to protect a town was to endow it with the supernatural charge of a saint's relics, so was it the ambition of her nephew to transform the whole of England into a bastion of holiness. As early as 925, two years before the conquest of York, a Mercian scribe had been hailing him as a man 'charged with the ordering of our entire Christian household, even to the whirlpools of the surging Ocean'.[7] Then, after joining Northumbria to his kingdom south of the Humber, Athelstan had been visited by a dream, self-evidently heaven-sent, and commanded to preserve the memory of the saints of the entire island. Where he could, he spoke to eyewitnesses of those martyred for their faith by the heathen. Most saints, though, like Cuthbert and Oswald, were long dead; and Athelstan, in searching out their relics, was actively seeking to fan the embers of their cults, so that the resulting blaze, illumining the darkness that for so many decades had shrouded Britain, might serve to keep the heathen permanently at bay. His ambition for his kingdom was that it should serve as a beacon to the world. 'Through the entire breadth of the three-quartered globe the fiery brilliance of the Holy Breath blows.' Such was the ringing proclamation made in 928, following Athelstan's return in triumph from the River Eamont. 'Manifold and inspiring are the gifts by which the taint of mortal wickedness is consumed.'[8]

1. A silver coin portraying Alfred, Athelstan's grandfather, worthily called 'the Great'.

2. The Alfred Jewel. Found in 1693, it bears the inscription 'Alfred ordered me to be made'. If, as seems likely, it originally adorned a pointer-stick used for reading, it constitutes a moving memorial to the great king's sponsorship of learning.

3. Edward, Athelstan's father. A warrior king of formidable achievement, his reign saw the forging of Wessex, Mercia and the Danelaw into something approximating to a unitary kingdom. This particular portrait imitates a coin, but is in fact a brooch.

4. The young Athelstan with his aunt, Æthelflæd. The statue was erected in the grounds of Tamworth Castle in 1913, to mark her founding of a *burh* on the site 1,000 years before.

5. The remains of Saint Oswald's Priory in Gloucester, where both Æthelflæd and her husband, Æthelred, were buried.

6. A silver coin from Æthelflæd's mint in Chester. The tower – either a church or the bulwark of a gate – symbolizes the project of urban regeneration that saw *burh*s built in a great line from the Mersey to Essex.

7. The coronation stone at Kingston upon Thames, where on 4 September 925 Athelstan was anointed, presented with a ring, a sword and a sceptre, and – a first in England – crowned.

8. Athelstan's conquest of York in 927 was the decisive moment in the forging of a unitary English kingdom. This coin, minted in the city soon after its capture, probably shows York Minster.

9. Athelstan, wearing his distinctive radiate crown, presents a book to Saint Cuthbert, in the frontispiece to Bede's life of the saint.

10. 'A dauntless folk'. This tenth-century illustration, which shows the Hebrews with their livestock, potently evokes the mingled ferocity and religiosity which characterized Athelstan's martial style.

11. Detail from a stole placed in Saint Cuthbert's tomb by Athelstan, complete with the name of Ælfflæd, Edward's second wife.

12. Otto the Great and his wife, Athelstan's half-sister Eadgyth.

13. Illustration from a psalter traditionally – and plausibly – believed to have been owned by Athelstan. He was renowned as *rex pius*: a most devout king.

14. *'REX TO BR'*, stamped after Athelstan's name on this silver coin, stands for *Rex Totius Britanniae*: 'the King of the Whole of Britain'. It was no idle boast.

15. Athelstan's tomb in Malmesbury.

So it was that Athelstan, even as he sought to pacify the furthermost reaches of the island by force of arms, also laboured hard to bring them into the light of Christ's Church. Bishops, whose numbers had been grievously culled during the upheavals of the previous half-century, were as important to Athelstan's purposes as ealdormen. In Northumbria he duly resurrected four sees that had fallen into ruin during the Viking occupation of the kingdom, and in the distant south-west established a separate bishopric for Cornwall. Dread of what demons might be lurking in the shadows of his realm had not been appeased by the oath that he had imposed upon his guests at Eamont 'to renounce all idolatry'.[9] In the wild places of Britain, beyond the churches and the priories that marked it out as a Christian land, there were still those who offered worship to Odin. Belief in the power of necromancy, though, was not confined to Vikings. The breaking of their kingdoms had left the task of dispelling the menace of the supernatural still incomplete. If the stories told by anxious priests were true, then there were plenty among Athelstan's own subjects who, in the hope of reading the future, would make offerings to wells, or trees, or stones. The unspeakable rituals of the heathen, who might think nothing of sacrificing a horse and then making sport with its phallus, were echoed in grim tales of Christian women transforming themselves into equine form, and revelling in the bestial.[10] Athelstan, who had not fought with the Vikings on the battlefield merely to see such practices flourish among his own people, sought to combat them as well he could. 'And so we have declared with regard to witchcraft, and sorcery, and deadly spells, that if it causes death, and the accused is unable to deny it, then his life shall be forfeit.'[11]

Nevertheless, sternly though Athelstan took his responsibilities as an anointed king, he did not scorn to moderate justice with compassion. Like Alfred, whose own law code had been prefaced with praise for 'the mercy taught by Christ',[12] he believed himself bound to legislate in a way that ranked as authentically Christian. The obligation on him to maintain the order of his kingdom and ensure the security of his subjects did not prevent him from fretting at the human cost. By primordial decree, it was the law in Wessex that even a child as young as ten might be condemned for theft; but Athelstan, in spelling out the details of what precisely was to constitute a capital offence, made sure to spare from execution all those under the age of thirteen. Nevertheless, his conscience remained troubled. Even as he sought to stamp out theft and robbery, legislating against them to an almost obsessive degree, anxiety that he might be betrayed by his own laws into savagery still gnawed at him. Lengthy consultations with his counsellors and his bishops duly persuaded him to ameliorate their strictness. 'The King thinks it cruel to have such young people put to death, and for such minor offences, as he has learnt is the common practice elsewhere. Therefore, it is the stated opinion both of the King and of those with whom he has discussed the matter that no one should be put to death who is under fifteen years of age.'[13] Clemency such as this was the reverse side of the ferocity with which Athelstan punished betrayals of his lordship. A Christian king was nothing, in his opinion, if he did not combine greatness with care for the vulnerable. In 932, on Christmas Eve, he duly marked the birth of his Saviour in a stable by issuing a charter that imposed a legal obligation upon its recipient to care for the poor. Other charters with similar stipulations then followed in a steady succession. Athelstan's determination that no one living on his own lands be permitted to starve saw him issue a particularly prescriptive ordinance. The officials responsible for his estates were warned by their master that fines would be levied on those who failed in their duty to the needy, and the proceeds donated to charity. 'My wish it is that you should always provide the destitute with food.'[14]

There was here, intermingled with the tone of command that came naturally to the greatest warrior of his age, the '*rex totius Britanniae*', a sense of urgency, of perturbation even. Athelstan, like his grandfather, never forgot that care for the wellbeing of his subjects was a charge that had been laid upon him directly by his Creator. Such a responsibility could hardly have been a more awesome one. No wonder, then, that Athelstan should have been as ready with legislation as he was with his sword. Even as his councils provided a forum in which he could make a show of all his greatness, they enabled him as well to acknowledge in public the manifold ills that afflicted his people. When, at the royal estate of Grateley in Hampshire, he convened 'a great assembly', complete with the Archbishop of Canterbury, 'and as many of the kingdom's chief and wisest men as he could gather',[15] Athelstan was making a pointed demonstration to all those in Wessex who might still resent him of his authority, his sway and his power; but he was also making law. The setting had been well chosen. To reach Grateley was to pass through thick forest, untamed by human hand, and to circle an ancient hill fort, from which pagan kings, long before the coming of the light of Christ to Britain, had once exercised their rule. Enthroned amid these reminders of the darkness that Christian kingship existed to keep at bay, Athelstan aimed to deliver a comprehensive range of solutions to the challenges faced by his subjects. From the administration of justice to the ordering of cattle-markets; from protecting the sanctity of churches to the functioning of the ordeal; from the maintenance of *burh*s to his familiar animadversions against robbery: all featured in the Grateley law code.

Naturally, in offering his prescriptions, Athelstan took for granted that the interests of his people were best served by the entrenchment and extension of his own rule. Between the setting of his assembly in a Hampshire glade and the vast scope of his recent conquests, there were inevitably tensions. Nothing better illustrated this than the provisions made at Grateley for regulating his kingdom's currency. In issuing them, Athelstan was legislating for the first time to enshrine a principle that was still far from universally accepted: his exclusive right to define what ranked as legal tender. Alfred himself, in the early years of his reign, had issued pennies jointly with the last legitimate king of Mercia, while Plegmund, his much-revered Archbishop of Canterbury, had not only minted coins but had them stamped with his own name. Meanwhile, beyond the limits of Alfred's realms, assorted pagan warlords had found the opportunities for self-promotion provided by maintaining a currency an aspect of Christian kingship that they were more than happy to emulate. At Grateley, though, with York conquered and Athelstan's claim to the rule of the *Angelcynn* now a fundamental part of his self-image, a new monetary order was proclaimed. 'There is to be one coinage throughout the King's dominion, and no one is to mint money except in a town.'[16] Just as England had been scoured clean of Viking rulers, so too was it to be scoured clean of their coins. Only those restamped with Athelstan's name were permitted still to circulate. There were to be no moneyers anywhere except for those directly under his licence. Yet even as this was being decreed at Grateley, the precise terms of the announcement hinted at the limits of his reach. In a clause that specified how many moneyers were to be licensed to each mint, mention of anywhere north of the Thames was notable by its absence. Athelstan's insistence that coins be minted exclusively in *burh*s, which saw them for the first time stamped as a matter of course with their place of issue, was as far as his direct control went. Only in southern Wessex did he exercise personal authority over the money supply. Elsewhere, in Mercia and in the lands conquered from the Vikings, coins still bore witness to the distinctive traditions of the one-time kingdoms in which they were being minted. The contours of Athelstan's greatness, so imposing to those who beheld him in his councils, might seem from a different vantage point considerably less substantial.

Dread of how fleeting might be their achievements, and of how unstable the foundations on which they had raised their kingdom, was precisely what had kept Alfred and his children so tireless in their labours, and so set never to cede ground; and so it was with Athelstan. Just as his resolve not to tolerate threats to his lordship had seen him strike deep into the Highlands, so did his anxiety at the failure of his laws to tame the ills of his kingdom prompt him to a degree of legislative activity unprecedented in the history of his people. One midwinter in particular, seated in Exeter surrounded by his councillors, he surveyed the state of his realm and was filled with despair. 'I, Athelstan the king, declare that I have learned how inadequately the public peace has been kept relative both to my wishes and to the provisions laid down at Grateley.'[17] His solution, inevitably, was to issue another raft of laws. It was the response of a man who believed, no less devoutly than his grandfather had done, in the potency of the written word. Endowed from his childhood 'with the holy eminence of learning', Athelstan had consecrated his entire reign to demonstrating the lesson taught him by Alfred's example: that the kingship of a Christian people required victories won in the *scriptorium* no less than on the battlefield.

This conviction was evident in the very language of his charters. Between 928 and 935, their penning was the responsibility, not of scribes employed as and when they might be required, but of a single and highly distinctive writer: one who very self-consciously aped the style of Athelstan's patron saint.[18] Aldhelm, a scholar who had died over two centuries previously, was the perfect model for anyone wishing to fashion a language appropriate to the newly united kingdom of the *Angelcynn*. Reputedly the brother of a West Saxon king, he had studied in Kent before becoming the Abbot of Malmesbury, a town where the ancient limits of Wessex met with those of Mercia. Long after his death, he was still being read with enthusiasm on both sides of the border. His distinctive prose style, elaborate, learned and difficult, had been adopted by Mercian scribes in the final century of their kingdom's independence as the epitome of good Latin, and made their own; Alfred, meanwhile, had been well known as an admirer of his poetry. Scribes in Edward's service, scouting around for a language that could rank as authentically Anglo-Saxon, had found Aldhelm ideally suited to their purpose, and duly begun to adorn royal charters with tags garnered from his writings. The saint's influence on Athelstan's chancery, though, was of a quite different magnitude. Document after document was produced in pitch-perfect imitation of Aldhelm's elevated prose. Their style was the perfect match for Athelstan's elevated conception of his kingship. Never before had there been charters to rival the sophistication and grandiosity of those issued in his name. All who listened to them being read out at court, concentrating in their effort to make sense of the archaic Latin, the occasional neologism, the intimidating flashes of Greek, could know themselves witness to a dazzling renaissance of scholarship.

Alfred would have been proud. The old king, explaining why he had set to translating Pope Gregory into English, had written in praise of 'the men of learning that had once existed among the *Angelcynn*', before the Viking firestorm had incinerated their monasteries and schools. Alfred, pledging himself to its resurrection, had been casting the future of his Anglo-Saxon kingdom, not as the bold innovation that it was but as the opposite: the fulfilment of the 'gesæliglica tida', the 'happy times', that had formerly existed. Athelstan too, who had brought the entirety of the *Angelcynn* into an unprecedented union, found in the legacy shared by his various subjects their common inheritance from an age 'before everything was ransacked and burned', a reassurance that he was doing nothing new. This was why, standing before the coffin of Cuthbert, he had presented the saint with books as well as gold and silver; and it was why, of all the many shrines to which he was devoted, 'he honoured none as more holy than Malmesbury',[19] where Aldhelm had his tomb. The land that England had formerly been, hallowed both by the sanctity of her saints and by the learning of her scholars, was what Athelstan wished his newly united kingdom to become. It was one, so he trusted, in which West Saxons and Mercians, Northumbrians and East Anglians, could all of them equally share. His goal it was to rule as a once and future king.

Yet even as Athelstan cast himself as a distinctively English ruler, heir to the inheritance of Bede, and Oswald, and Aldhelm, he never thought to abandon his broader ambitions. It was not enough, for a king who claimed the sway of Britain as well as of England, to rest content solely with the traditions of the *Angelcynn*. The power he aspired to exercise was of an imperial scope; and so it was important to his purposes, even as the ornate Latin of his charters provided them with a flavour of Malmesbury, that it endowed them as well with something of the palmy dignity of Rome.

In affecting the role of a British emperor, Athelstan's primary aim was, of course, to intimidate other kings and princes in the island; but he also had his eyes fixed on another, and more exacting, audience. Ever since the coronation of Charlemagne by the pope in 800, it was the kings of Francia who had provided the measure by which imperial greatness was judged. No ruler in the fragmented and Viking-harried island of Britain had ever come close to ranking as their peer. Although the last descendant of Charlemagne to claim the title of emperor had been deposed and blinded back in 905, and although the empire itself had split into eastern and western halves, its rulers remained the cynosures of Christian kingship. As a result, no sterner judges of Athelstan's pretensions could possibly have been imagined – and the *rex totius Britanniae* knew it.

Yet there was a sense in which the Frankish monarchy, far from serving him as a role model, had come to provide him instead with a grim and salutary warning. In contrast to his own united kingdom of the *Angelcynn*, Francia was palpably imploding. In the eastern half of the empire, the crown had passed into the hands of a man who was not even a Frank: Henry, the Duke of the Saxons. Meanwhile, in the western half, rival magnates snarled and snapped at each other, and carved out dominions for themselves that rendered its monarchy increasingly spectral. The scent of blood, not surprisingly, had set the nostrils of predators flaring. Vikings from the North – 'North Men' – had planted a colony on the shores of the Channel, called after them 'Normandy'; heathens from beyond the Elbe raided the monasteries and churches of the Saxons; pagan horsemen named the Hungarians, 'of disgusting aspect, with deep-set eyes and short stature',[20] ravaged Bavaria. To the ambitious and upstart dukes of the beleaguered Frankish Empire, the kingdom ruled by Athelstan, far from seeming contemptible, could hardly strike them as other than enviably stable and secure. Even before his accession to the throne, and his conquest of Northumbria, one of his half-sisters had already been reckoned worthy of the most prestigious match in Christendom. Shortly after Edward's conquest of the Danelaw in 917, his daughter Eadgifu had been married to none other than Charles III, King of West Francia and lineal descendant of Charlemagne himself. Although she had been quick to bear her husband a son, named by his parents Louis, disaster had struck soon afterwards. Charles, an incompetent and shifty ruler, had been deposed in 922 and immured for good the following year; Eadgifu, rather than risk losing her infant son, had promptly sent him for protection across the Channel to her father. Athelstan, succeeding to the responsibility for the prince's upbringing, had been able to glory in having a descendant of Charlemagne as his ward.

Further proofs of the high regard with which the house of Cerdic had come to be regarded by the elite of Francia were quick to follow. Athelstan, possessed as he was of an enormous brood of sisters, was ideally placed to capitalize on the need of ambitious princes in the Frankish Empire to burnish their status; and he duly made sure to do so. First to be sent across the Channel was his half-sister, Ealdhild. In 926 she was married by Athelstan to the most powerful man in West Francia: the aptly nicknamed Hugh the Great.

Turning down the throne which his own father, following the deposition of Charles III, had briefly held until his death in battle, Hugh had made use of the chaos of the times to carve out an immense fiefdom between the Seine and the Loire. As wealthy as he was powerful, he had been able to present Athelstan with a dowry of such splendour that the memory of it was still inspiring rhapsodies centuries later. The spear of Charlemagne; the lance which had pierced the side of Christ; 'a small piece of the holy and wonderful Cross enclosed in crystal':[21] treasures worthy of an emperor indeed. Embellished in the retelling though the precise details of the gifts sent by Hugh may well have been, it is evident that they were sufficient to secure Athelstan's reputation among his subjects as owner of 'the greatest of relic-collections, gathered far and wide'.[22] Even this, however, was not the limit of the prestige that Athelstan proved capable of securing for himself from abroad. In 929, another of his sisters, Eadgyth, was married to the most eligible prince in Christendom: the eldest son of Henry, the King of East Francia. Otto, fearless, charismatic and intimidatingly hairy, was a man very much of Athelstan's stamp; and the bonds of kinship between the two dynasties, Saxon both, were powerfully cemented by the queenly bearing and diligent saintliness of Eadgyth. When Otto, in 936, finally succeeded his father, it was to a realm that had come to bear more than a passing resemblance to Athelstan's own united kingdom of the *Angelcynn*: 'a great and far-spreading dominion, not handed down to him by his forefathers, but won instead by his own exertions, and bestowed upon him by God alone'.[23]

Perhaps it was only to be expected, with rebellion across Britain seemingly tamed, and the house of Cerdic joined by marriage to the two most powerful men beyond the Channel, that Athelstan should increasingly have focused his attention on the continent. Shortly before Otto's coronation in the late summer of 936, another prince had been anointed and crowned in Francia: Louis, the still youthful son of Charles III. It was Hugh the Great, manoeuvring to frustrate his rivals, who had invited the young man back; but Athelstan, despatching Louis with an armed retinue and a picked escort of bishops, was hardly reluctant to see his nephew installed on the West Frankish throne. The policy of fostering foreign princes, and schooling them in the arts required to rule a kingdom, was one on which he had always been keen. Louis was certainly not the only ward to have been adopted by him. Others raised in Athelstan's court included Haakon, youngest son of the most powerful warlord in Scandinavia, and Alain, heir to the dukedom of Brittany, which the Vikings had wrested from his father some three decades previously. Athelstan, once Constantin and the other fractious kings of the North had been brought to heel in 934, had actively sought to expand his influence beyond the limits of Britain by assisting his wards to reclaim their various patrimonies. Haakon, steeled by the faith in which he had been raised by his foster-father, had been sent with ships and men to seize the western shoreline of Scandinavia, and emerged to rule it as the first Christian king of Norway. Then, in 936, the same year that saw the return of Louis to West Francia, Athelstan sponsored a second expedition across the Channel.

Alain, a warrior of such proficiency that, rather than hunt bears with a spear, he preferred instead to brain them with a wooden staff, succeeded in seizing back his inheritance from the Vikings and sweeping them into the sea. Athelstan could feel well pleased. Norway, Francia, Brittany: the seaboard facing his kingdom was now almost completely ruled by men tied to him by bonds of family and obligation. Never before, it seemed, had his rule been so secure. Never before had his greatness been so apparent.

But it turned out that he had over-reached himself. Distracted by his focus on overseas, he had failed to keep track of the secret schemings in his rear: the messengers travelling to and fro between Alba, the banks of the Clyde and Dublin. Constantin, determined still, despite his grudging submission in 934, to shake off the yoke of his overlord; Owain, fearful of what the greatness of the emergent English kingdom on his doorstep might mean for his own much smaller realm; Olaf, unreconciled to his father's loss of York: Athelstan had underestimated them all. Two centuries later, when a history of his reign came to be written, it would be reported that the realization of his blindness had numbed him. Brought the news of the powers ranged against him, he had acted at first as though frozen by the sheer horror of it. As harvests in the north of his kingdom were put to the torch and peasants fled before the onslaught, so the *rex totius Britanniae* had seemed to shrink from acting. 'But at length the cries of complaint stirred the King. He knew it insufferable to be branded with the shame of having submitted meekly to barbarian arms.'[24] And so, with the weariness of a man who had believed his life's great labour of construction completed, only to find it threatened with utter ruin, he had marshalled his troops, led them northwards, ridden to Brunanburh.

Whether the memory of Athelstan's initial hesitation before his most celebrated campaign was an authentic one or not, it is clear enough that the devastation wrought by the terrible battle was hardly confined to the ranks of the defeated. The aftermath of Brunanburh was not what Constantin or Owain might most have dreaded. Athelstan did not pursue them. He did not ravage their lands. He did not enforce renewed oaths of submission at the point of his sword. Instead, rather than continue northwards from the battlefield, beyond the lands of the *Angelcynn* into the heartlands of his vanquished foes, he turned and headed back to Wessex. Athelstan had sustained grievous losses of his own. With him as he rode south were brought the corpses of two of his cousins, the sons of his uncle Æthelweard, fallen amid the carnage at Brunanburh.[25] They were buried not at Winchester, but beside the tomb of Saint Aldhelm in Malmesbury, on either side of the altar. It was as though, after their deaths in a battle that had seen West Saxons and Mercians fight side by side as one, Athelstan had wanted for their final resting place a site that would speak clearly of the cause for which they had fallen: the united kingdom forged by Alfred, and Edward, and Æthelflæd, and to which he himself had devoted his entire life.

'All things fail, and the world itself is dissolving into terminal ruin. Therefore must we make speed to those fields of delight the joy of which lies beyond description.'[26] This reflection, composed in the inimitable style of Aldhelm and issued in Athelstan's name shortly before Christmas in 935, might have seemed an unduly pessimistic assertion to make in the charter of a king who had fashioned and achieved so much. The shock of Brunanburh, though, had provided a salutary reminder of how precarious were the affairs of mere mortal kingdoms. Athelstan had survived the test of that terrible battle, and emerged from it with his reputation only further burnished – and yet how perilously close to 'terminal ruin' his many labours had indeed been brought. Back in Wessex from the Brunanburh campaign, he continued to shoulder all the manifold responsibilities of kingship: touring his realm, issuing charters and administering justice, engaging in foreign affairs. The strain of it, though, was very great. On 27 October 939, while still only in his mid-forties, Athelstan died in Gloucester. His body, rather than being laid to rest beside his aunt's tomb in the priory of Saint Oswald, or taken to join that of his father in Winchester, was brought to Malmesbury. There he was buried under the altar, 'next to holy Aldhelm'.[27] Meanwhile, across the island he had so put in his shadow, and across the islands that lay beyond it too, the news of his death rapidly spread. There were many, of course, who greeted it with relief: in Alba, and in Northumbria, where it would soon become all too apparent just how grudging its leaders' acceptance of Athelstan's dominance had always been, and on the ships of Viking adventurers. Such restlessness, though, expressing itself as it did only on his death, was its own compliment: due acknowledgement of the awe and dread that he had struck into his foes, and of the greatness that he won for himself. His own country-men understood this; and so too did those who marked his passing from afar. A scribe in Ulster, recording the death of Athelstan, certainly had no doubts as to the stature of the King of the *Angelcynn*. He had been, so the chronicler declared, nothing less than 'the roof-tree of the dignity of the western world'.[28]

Malmesbury

Some two centuries after Athelstan had been laid to rest in Malmesbury, his tomb was briefly opened and his mortal remains exposed to view. A monk from the abbey, taking the chance to inspect them, was able to corroborate reports of the celebrated king's stature: that he had been of average height and slender build. Not everything in the coffin, though, was bones. Traces of hair were still to be seen – and this too the monk studied attentively. 'It had been', so he recorded later, 'blonde in colour, and beautifully twisted into golden braids.'[1]

William of Malmesbury had good reason to take an interest in such details. Born in Wiltshire, a county for which Athelstan had always shown an especial fondness, and sent to the abbey as a child, he had grown up with a justifiable pride in the achievements of the king who lay buried there. It was thanks to the generosity of their most celebrated patron that the monks of Malmesbury could boast of a particularly awesome relic: the fragment of the True Cross sent long before as a dowry payment by Hugh the Great. William's horizons, though, were far from bound by the limits of his monastery. Fascinated by the past since a child, it was his ambition to write a history of

England that might stand comparison with Bede's. That one of his parents was actually a Norman did not in any way inhibit him from declaring his motivation to be 'love of my country'.[2] The sheer antiquity of the English state, far from being despised by its conquerors, tended instead to be both prized and respected by them, for it added lustre to their rule. A Norman anointed as *rex Anglorum*, no matter that his native tongue was French, ruled as the heir of those same kings who had first, long before the slaughter at Hastings, fashioned England and brought it into being. William, whose sophistication as a historian was profound, appreciated better than anyone the full scale of their achievements. It was not only their victories in war that had laid the foundations of the English state, but their concern for justice and their sponsorship of learning. Generous a patron of Malmesbury though Athelstan had been, there were reasons far more telling why William should have portrayed him as the greatest of England's kings. 'The opinion of the English that he governed them with a greater concern for law and for education than anyone else in their history is a valid one.'[3]

By the time that William wrote this, 'Englalonde' had been a term in common use for a century, and its lineaments as a kingdom come to be taken widely for granted. It was evident as well that the roots of this precociously unitary state, with its single currency, its common language and its intimidating monarchy, reached back in turn a further century – and that the first man who could legitimately be reckoned its king was Athelstan. 'Through God's grace he ruled all of England alone which before him many kings held among themselves.'[4] Yet at the time of his death, it would not have been at all clear that the kingdom he had fashioned and defended so untiringly over the course of his reign would hold together now that he was gone. There were those alive, after all, who had been born at a time when the fate of Wessex itself still hung in the balance. To fear for the future of the united kingdom of the *Angelcynn* in the wake of Athelstan's death, and to anticipate its disintegration, was not to doubt the scale of his achievements, but rather to pay them their proper due. 'Glorious king, holy champion of the Church, bringer of the evil heathen into the dust, pattern for your subjects, model of all virtues, scatterer of your foes, father of your priests, helper of the destitute, lover of all the saints, interlocutor of the angels.'[5] How could Athelstan's heirs possibly hope to measure up to such a paragon?

Sure enough, in the immediate wake of his death the darkest fears of his followers appeared realized. No sooner had news reached Dublin that the victor of Brunanburh was no more, than Olaf Guthfrithsson was heading back across the Irish Sea. This time there was no one to stop him. He marched directly on York. Its gates were opened. The city's elite threw itself into active collaboration. Particularly enthusiastic was Wulfstan, York's archbishop, whose resentment of West Saxon rule far outweighed any distaste that he might have felt for a pagan warlord. By the spring of 940, the new king of York and his archbishop were both riding southwards at the head of an invasion force. War returned to Mercia. Tamworth was stormed and stripped bare, and a large chunk of territory south of the Humber extorted by treaty. Towns conquered by Edward and Æthelflæd more than two decades previously were surrendered to Olaf. Leicester and Lincoln, Nottingham and Derby: all were returned to Viking rule.

It might have seemed a mortal blow to the integrity of the Anglo-Saxon kingdom – but in the event was to prove only a glancing wound. Edmund, whose succession to Athelstan had been a notably smooth one, and marked by none of the tensions that traditionally in Wessex had accompanied the accession of a new king, was a precociously seasoned warrior. Although still only eighteen when crowned, he was already the veteran of two major campaigns: for he had ridden by the side of his half-brother during both the invasion of Alba and the Brunanburh campaign. The unexpected death of Olaf in 941 gave him his opportunity to embark on a headlong process of reconquest. By 942, everywhere south of the Humber was back under his rule. By 944 he had retaken York. The following year saw him plant his banner on the banks of the Clyde, force the King of the Cumbrians into a humiliating submission and blind two of his sons as punishment for their father's treachery. Even now, though, Edmund could not rest entirely secure. Viking adventurers still lurked on the margins, awaiting their chance. In 946, when Edmund was stabbed to death in a brawl, the protracted scavenging over Northumbria entered what was to prove its final phase. Once again, a Viking warlord seized control of York. Once again, a son of Edward embarked on a campaign of pacification north of the Humber. Eadred was the youngest of Athelstan's half-brothers – and Eadred it was, crowned in succession to Edmund, who would finally succeed in making his dynasty's rule of Northumbria permanent. In 952, Wulfstan, the ever-slippery archbishop who had long served as York's kingmaker, was arrested by Eadred's agents and packed off south to become the Bishop of Dorchester. Two years later, amid remote and windswept moorland, the last Viking king of York fell in battle. Never again would the city serve as a royal capital. The prospect of an independent Northumbria was at an end.

A momentous development – and ripe with implications for more than 'Englalonde'. The kings who followed Athelstan had not forgotten his claim to rule as lord of the whole of Britain. Edmund and Eadred were both seduced by it; and so too was Edgar, the younger son of Edmund who in 959, after the brief but troubled reign of his elder brother, Eadwig, succeeded to the English throne. It was not enough for the heirs of Athelstan to rule merely as the *rex Anglorum*. In 973, fourteen years after becoming king, Edgar was crowned amid the aptly imperial surroundings of what had once been Roman Bath, and hailed by those present as the pre-eminent king of Britain. The echo of the great assembly held by his uncle at Cirencester some forty years previously was palpable – and no doubt deliberate. Nevertheless, the contrasts too were telling. Whereas Athelstan had been attended in person by Welsh princes and the kings of Alba and Strathclyde, Edgar's consecration at Bath was witnessed by an altogether more circumscribed audience: 'the nobility of the English'.[6] That he then headed from his coronation to Chester, there to meet six kings summoned from the rest of Britain, only emphasized the clear distinction that had come to exist since Athelstan's time between the English-speaking regions of the island and the realms elsewhere. Edgar, who made sure to arrive on the River Dee escorted by his entire fleet, could hardly have struck a more imposing figure; and his six guests, duly overawed, 'all swore solemn oaths that they would be his allies by sea and land'.[7] The paradox, though, was already evident: that the more solidly the foundations of an English state were cemented together, so the harder did it become to present the island as a single realm.

Seen in this light, Athelstan's conquest of York, the feat which had first served to project the power of the West Saxon monarchy deep into the north of Britain, can be seen as the decisive event in the making of Scotland as well as of England. There was certainly nothing preordained about the emergence of either kingdom. Had Athelstan neglected to seize his chance in 927, then the political contours of Britain might easily have ended up very different. It is not far-fetched to imagine an Anglo-Viking kingdom ruled from York putting down permanent roots. The heirs of Alfred would then have been confined to Southumbria, and the kings of Alba to the Highlands. As it was, the absorption of Northumbria into the emergent kingdom of England gave the Scots the chance to extend their own sway. Already, in Athelstan's reign, the sheer scale of the effort required to ravage the Highlands had demonstrated the challenge that any West Saxon king was bound to face in exercising lordship over lands some five hundred miles north of Wessex. Edmund, after his own ravaging of

Strathclyde, had no choice but to entrust it to the overlord-ship of the King of the Scots, 'upon these terms – that the King of the Scots should help him by land and sea'.[8] This oath, though, was not long upheld. When an English gar-rison was obliged soon afterwards to evacuate the Northumbrian stronghold of Edinburgh, Scottish rule was entrenched for the first time south of the Forth. A century on, and it extended almost to Lindisfarne. The inhabitants of Lothian, for all that they might still regard themselves as English, were no longer subject to an English king. Instead, they had been brought to acknowledge the lord-ship of another man: the ruler of a kingdom that they would call, in their own language, 'Scotland'.

This division of Britain into rival kingdoms, by the time that William of Malmesbury sat down to write his history, was coming to seem the natural state of affairs. Two hun-dred years on from Athelstan's conquest of York, memories were fading of the seismic character of his reign, and of just how momentous its effect had been upon the political configuration of the island. 'He was a man whose life, though short, was glorious.'[9] William, in delivering this verdict, was as influenced by what he understood to have been Athelstan's character as he was by the great king's martial achievements. Piety, learning, a passion for justice: such were the qualities that particularly drew his praise. How, though, at such a remove from his subject, could William be confident that his portrait of Athelstan was an accurate one? He did not duck the question. For his history of the great king, so William declared, he had been able to draw upon a remarkable find: 'an ancient volume'[10] uncovered during the course of his researches and written in a notably florid style during the lifetime of Athelstan himself. This claim, although most scholars accept its veracity, has proven impossible to substantiate – for of the 'ancient volume' there is today no trace. As a result, the challenge of squaring William's portrait of Athelstan with the sparse details that can be garnered from the king's own lifetime has proven a treacherous one for historians to meet.[11] Had the book only survived, then we might have had in our possession an inestimable prize: a biography fit to compare with Asser's life of Alfred, written by a contemporary and full of intimate detail. As it is, compared to his grandfather, Athelstan is doomed to appear an altogether more elusive and indistinct figure. In a country that has been a unitary state for longer than any other in Europe, the sheer feat of statecraft that was required to bring it into existence risks being signally underestimated. The king who founded England has largely been forgotten even by the English.

Nothing better illustrates the oblivion that has largely claimed his reputation than the fact that the very site of Brunanburh long ago slipped from memory. That a glorious victory had been won there was celebrated by a poet writing – to judge by the prominence given in its opening lines to 'Edmund *ætheling*' – some time in the reign of Athelstan's brother; but it is impossible to pinpoint from the poem where precisely the battle was fought. The details that it does provide are sufficient to pique curiosity – but they are inadequate to satisfy it. They make it evident that Constantin, escaping the scene of his defeat, was able to withdraw to Alba; that Olaf, similarly taking flight, 'sought Dublin over deep water';[12] and that Athelstan, triumphing over his foes, had done so 'defending his own land'.[13] A further pointer is provided by a chronicler writing some thirty years after the battle, who records it as having been fought, not at Brunanburh, but at '*Brunandun*' – 'the hill of Brune'.[14] Since it is the perennial ambition of historians, as William of Malmesbury long ago recognized, 'to bring to light things lost in the midden of the past',[15] it is hardly surprising that these few vague details should have prompted a startlingly wide array of theories as to the likeliest site of the battle – nor that there should remain to this day a notable lack of consensus. Perhaps Athelstan won his great victory at Bromborough on the Wirral – and yet, despite the resemblance of the town's name to 'Brunanburh', and the fact that Cheshire had been settled by Vikings from Ireland since the time of Æthelflæd, what would a king of Alba have been doing on a peninsula so far south? Perhaps, then, based on the evidence of a twelfth-century chronicle, the battle was fought beside the Humber – but would a king of Dublin really have sailed the whole way round Britain to launch his invasion? What, then, of the ancient hill fort of Brunswark in what is now Dumfriesshire, but was then a part of the kingdom of Strathclyde? Like Bromborough, its name seems to echo that of Brunanburh; unlike Bromborough, the site does actually feature a hill. Again, though, not all the pieces fit: for Athelstan, if he had indeed won his victory there, deep within an adversary's lands, would hardly have been described a few years later as 'defending his own land'. Based on the fact that both Olaf and Constantin were able to escape the battle, and that it was fought on English territory beside a hill, the likeliest location for Brunanburh would appear to be somewhere west of the Pennines, within easy reach both of the sea and of the Cumbrian frontier – but more than that it is hard to say.

None of which detracts, of course, from the decisive role played by the great victory in ensuring that the kingdom of the *Angelcynn* would stay united – nor from the scale of what was achieved by the victor himself. The site of Brunanburh may be unrecoverable; but the implications of what was fashioned by Athelstan and his dynasty more than a millennium ago have lately come to possess a renewed saliency. As the bonds weaken that for the past three hundred years have joined England and Scotland in a united kingdom, so inevitably have the English as well as the Scots begun to ponder what defines them as a nation. That a union as long-lasting as that of Great Britain might fray can hardly help but serve as a reminder that the joining of different peoples in a shared sense of identity is not something easily achieved and maintained. Perhaps we can see now, in a way that we could not even a few decades ago, just how astonishing the creation of 'Englalonde' actually was. The story of how, over the course of three generations, the royal dynasty of Wessex went from near-oblivion to fashioning a kingdom that still endures today is the most remarkable and momentous in British history. That Athelstan, let alone Edward and Ætheflæd, are perforce shadowy figures, with inner lives that are as unknowable to us as the site of Brunanburh, does not render their accomplishments any the less astonishing. They and Alfred richly merit being commemorated as England's founding fathers – or, of course, in Æthelflæd's case, as England's founding mother.

Some two and a half decades after the death of Athelstan, a bishop at the court of King Edgar, surveying his sway over 'the whole dominion of England', hailed it as a miracle, 'obtained by God's grace'.[16] Yet Æthelwold, who had served as one of Athelstan's closest advisers before becoming a priest, knew full well that the united kingdom of the English had been obtained by human agency as well as by divine providence. Even as he expressed his astonishment that the land ruled over by Edgar should be marked by such prosperity and peace, he did not hesitate to give credit to the young king's forebears, who had wrought so much in the teeth of such terrible odds. 'Mature in age and very prudent, and farseeing in wisdom, and hard to overcome in any strife': such praise, coming from a man who had grown up by Athelstan's side and witnessed the ferocious burdens placed on him by his kingship, carries rare conviction. Bishop Æthelwold spoke for all those who, enjoying the order brought to lands that only decades before had been scenes of carnage and devastation, felt due gratitude for what had been achieved by Alfred and his heirs. He, close enough in time to Athelstan's reign to have been the great king's protégé, understood the full scale of his debt. We, at a millennium's remove, could perhaps remember it better.

Notes

BRUNANBURH

1. The phrase is Æthelweard's: '*bellum ... magnum*' (4.5).
2. *Anglo-Saxon Chronicle* (E), entry for 937.
3. The charter which gives us the date of Athelstan's coronation titles him '*rex Saxonum et Anglorum*': 'King of the Saxons and the Angles'.
4. *The Gothic History of Jordanes* 25, trans. Charles C. Mierow (Princeton: Princeton University Press, 1915).
5. 'Ethologically speaking ... it is very probable that ravens and wolves learned to associate groups of armed men with food, and that they appeared before the fighting broke out.' ('Birds and Bird-lore in the Literature of Anglo-Saxon England' [unpublished PhD thesis], by Mohamed Eric Rahman Lacey, p. 118.) Lacey's argument that ravens in the early medieval period had learned to follow armies as a matter of course is as intriguing as it is ultimately convincing.
6. Spoken by Paulinus, the missionary to the Northumbrians, and first Bishop of York. *Life of Gregory the Great*, 15.
7. Snorri Sturluson, *The Deluding of Gylfi*, 38, in *The Prose Edda: Norse Mythology*, trans. Jesse L. Byock (London: Penguin, 2005).
8. *Hrafnsmál*, 8.21, quoted by Neil Price, *The Viking Way* (Uppsala: University of Uppsala Press, 2002), p. 367.
9. *Njál's Saga*, 157, quoted in ibid., p. 333. The verses are from a poetic interpolation in the saga, and ostensibly refer to the Battle of Clontarf, which was fought outside Dublin in 1014. They have been dated convincingly, however, to a battle that took place in Ireland almost a century earlier, within the lifetimes of those who fought at Brunanburh. See R. G. Poole, *Viking Poems on War and Peace: A Study in Skaldic Narrative* (Toronto: Toronto University Press, 1991), pp. 120–24.
10. MS Cotton Tiberius A.ii, fol. 15r (British Library), line 1.
11. 'Battle of Brunanburh', *Anglo-Saxon Chronicle* (A): entry for 937, p. 35–6.
12. Ibid., 45–6.
13. Æthelweard (4.5).
14. 'Battle of Brunanburh', 65–71.

I. WESSEX

1. Æthelwold, 1.1.
2. *Anglo-Saxon Chronicle* (D), entry for 189.
3. Gildas, *The Ruin of Britain*, 24.1.

4. A translation by Simon Keynes and Michael Lapidge in *Alfred the Great: Asser's Life of King Alfred and Other Contemporary Sources* (London: Penguin, 1983) of Alfred's translation of Boethius' *Consolation of Philosophy*, p. 136.

5. Bede, 1.22. *Ecclesiastical History of the English People*, trans. Leo Sherley-Price, revised by R. E. Latham (London: Penguin, 1990).

6. Æthelweard, 1.3.

7. *Anglo-Saxon Chronicle* (E), entry for 592. In point of fact, Gregory became pope in 590.

8. Bede, 3.1.

9. Adomnán, 1.1. *Life of St Columba*, trans. Richard Sharpe (London: Penguin, 1995).

10. Bede, 3.13.

11. *Anglo-Saxon Chronicle* (B & C), entry for 855.

12. Psalm 2.6 (adapted), from Alfred's prose translation of the Psalter (Keynes and Lapidge, p. 154).

13. Asser, 76.

14. King Alfred, Preface to his translation of Saint Gregory's *Regula Pastoralis*.

15. Samuel 1: 16.13.

16. *Anglo-Saxon Chronicle* (E), entry for 878.

17. Asser, 42.

18. Æthelweard, 4.3.

19. King Alfred's will; Keynes and Lapidge, p. 175.

20. Quoted by Richard Abels, *Alfred the Great: War, Kingship and Culture in Anglo-Saxon England* (London: Longman, 1998), p. 60.

21. The complete poem is reproduced in Michael Lapidge, 'Some Latin Poems as Evidence for the Reign of Athelstan', *Anglo-Saxon England* 9 (1980), p. 71. Most scholars accept that it provides contemporary confirmation of what Geoffrey of Monmouth, in his account of the investiture, anachronistically refers to as a 'knighting' (2.133) – although, as is invariably the case with historians of Anglo-Saxon England, there is the odd exception.

22. Asser, Dedication.

2. MERCIA

1. *Anglo-Saxon Chronicle* (A), entry for 900.

2. Admittedly, it is nowhere explicitly stated in the sources that Æthelhelm had predeceased Alfred – but the fact that he does not feature in accounts of Æthelwold's rebellion makes it almost certain.

3. The detail that Æthelwold married the nun derives from much later writers, but seems to preserve an authentic memory: marriage without royal permission was a popular way in the tenth century for princely rebels to proclaim their defiance of a king. Alex Woolf, in an essay in *The Defence of Wessex: The Burghal Hidage and the Anglo-Saxon Fortifications*, ed. D. Hill and A. Rumble (Manchester: Manchester University Press, 1996), pp. 98–9, floats the intriguing possibility that the nun may have been Alfred's daughter, Ælfgifu, the Abbess of Shaftesbury.

4. It has been suggested (e.g. by Sarah Foot, *Æthelstan: The First King of England* [New Haven and London: Yale University Press, 2011], p. 37) that Ælfflæd was

the daughter of the ealdorman of Wiltshire, also called Æthelhelm, on the grounds that 'the Church's teaching on consanguineous marriages would have ruled out a union between first cousins'. Not only were Edward and Ælfflæd second cousins, though, but Edward, judging by his readiness to marry and then dispose of wives, seems to have been as flexible in his attitude to marriage as were many other kings in the tenth century. The crisis-racked circumstances of Edward's second marriage make Ælfflæd's identity almost certain: she was of royal blood.

5. Asser, 77.

6. William of Malmesbury, 2.133. (*Gesta Regum Anglorum*, vol. 1, ed. R. A. B. Mynors, R. M. Thomson and M. Winterbottom [Oxford: Oxford University Press, 1998].)

7. Almost all scholars have accepted the tradition first recorded by William of Malmesbury that Athelstan was brought up in Mercia. For a countervailing view, see David Dumville's collection of essays, *Wessex and England: From Alfred to Edgar* (Woodbridge: Boydell Press, 1992), p. 146.

8. From the poem reproduced in Lapidge, p. 71. See n. 20 to ch. 1 for the likely dating.

9. The suggestion is Frank Stenton's; see *Anglo-Saxon England* (Oxford: Oxford University Press, 1943), p. 322.

10. Æthelweard, 4.4.

11. From *The Annals of Ireland: Three Fragments*. Quoted by F. T. Wainwright, 'Æthelflæd, Lady of the Mercians', in *Scandinavian England: Collected Papers* (Chichester: Phillimore, 1975), p. 83.

12. *The Mercian Register.*

13. Æthelweard, 4.4.

14. From a paraphrase of a lost charter issued in the first year of Athelstan's reign. Quoted by Foot, *Æthelstan*, p. 34.

15. *Annals of Ulster*, ed. Séan Mac Airt & Gearóid Mac Niocaill (Dublin: Dublin Institute for Advanced Studies, 1983), p. 368.

16. *Anglo-Saxon Chronicle* (A), entry for 917.

17. William of Malmesbury, 2.125.

18. Ibid., 2.133.

3. NORTHUMBRIA

1. William of Malmesbury, 2.137.

2. *Anglo-Saxon Chronicle* (A), entry for 886.

3. Such, at any rate, is the current consensus on what is termed 'the Second Anglo-Saxon Ordo'. See Janet Nelson, 'The First Use of the Second Anglo-Saxon Ordo', in *Myth, Rulership, Church and Charters*, ed. Julia Barrow and Andrew Wareham (Aldershot: Ashgate, 2008).

4. Any attempt to extrapolate from the minimal evidence available a thesis as to Athelstan's sexuality would be as anachronistic as it was nugatory.

5. The phrasing of the *Anglo-Saxon Chronicle*'s account of this summit implies that it may have been held in the Peak District, where Edward had just built a fortress at Bakewell.

6. *Anglo-Saxon Chronicle* (A), entry for 920.

7. *Anglo-Saxon Charters: An Annotated List and Bibliography*, ed. Peter Sawyer (London: Royal Historical Society, 1968), p. 395.
8. Alcuin, quoted by Sarah Foot in 'The Making of *Angelcynn*: English Identity Before the Norman Conquest', *Transactions of the Royal Historical Society* 6 (1996), p. 29.
9. *Anglo-Saxon Chronicle* (D), entry for 927.
10. *Armes Prydein Vawr*, line 18.
11. 1 *Athelstan* 5.
12. Sawyer, p. 416.
13. Folcuin, *Acts of the Abbey of St-Bertin*, 107.
14. From an inscription in a gospel book presented to Christ Church, Canterbury.
15. Radbod, Abbot of Dol, to Athelstan, in *English Historical Documents*, vol. 1: *c. 500–1042*, ed. Dorothy Whitelock (London: Eyre & Spottiswoode, 1968), p. 228.

4. *ANGELCYNN*

1. *Anglo-Saxon Chronicle* (D), entry for 793.
2. *History of Saint Cuthbert*, ch. 13.
3. Ibid., ch. 23.
4. Ibid.
5. The precise date of this story is much debated, but in light of its relevance to Athelstan's self-image, and the evidence for a possible origin of the story in the reign of Alfred himself (see Mechtild Gretsch, *Ælfric and the Cult of Saints in Late Anglo-Saxon England* [Cambridge: Cambridge University Press, 2009], pp. 78–82), it is reasonable to assume that a version of it, at the very least, was current in 934.
6. *History of Saint Cuthbert*, ch. 16. *Historia de Sancto Cuthberto: A History of Saint Cuthbert and a Record of His Patrimony*, ed. Ted Johnson South (Cambridge: D. S. Brewer, 2002).
7. Sawyer, p. 395.
8. Ibid., p. 399.
9. *Anglo-Saxon Chronicle* (D), entry for 927.
10. See Price, p. 219.
11. 2 *Athelstan* 6.
12. *Alfred* 49.7.
13. 6 *Athelstan* 12.1.
14. *Ordinance Relating to Charities.*
15. From the Epilogue to the Latin version of 2 *Athelstan*.
16. 2 *Athelstan* 14.
17. Preamble to 5 *Athelstan*.
18. See Ben Snook, *The Anglo-Saxon Chancery: The History, Language and Production of Anglo-Saxon Charters from Alfred to Edgar* (Woodbridge: Boydell Press, 2015), pp. 107–11, for a convincing demonstration that 'Athelstan A', as he is known by scholars, was most likely Ælfwine, the Bishop of Lichfield.
19. William of Malmesbury, 2.136.
20. Otto of Freising, *The Two Cities*, trans. C. C. Mierow (New York: Columbia University Press, 1928), p. 66.

21. William of Malmesbury, 2.135.

22. From the Exeter relic list; cited by Patrick W. Conner in *Anglo-Saxon Exeter: A Tenth-Century Cultural History* (Woodbridge: Boydell Press, 1993), p. 177.

23. Widukind, 1.41. *Res Gestae Saxonicae*, in *Monumenta Germaniae Historica: Scriptores* (Hanover, 1838).

24. William of Malmesbury, 135. Although William wrote in the twelfth century, his claim to have drawn for his account of Athelstan's life on a tenth-century source has recently, after the sustained criticism of Lapidge (1980), come back into favour, largely thanks to the advocacy of Wood. Foot, in her biography of Athelstan (pp. 251–8), provides the best survey. On William's reliability as a source for the Brunanburh campaign, see Michael Wood, *In Search of England: Journeys into the English Past* (London: Penguin, 1999): '[t]his passage is clearly no flight of fancy. The idea that Athelstan of all people could be criticized for lassitude and complacency is inconceivable as a forgery of the twelfth century . . .'

25. So, at any rate, William of Malmesbury reports (2.135). His familiarity with the necropolis at Malmesbury being what it was, it seems improbable that he would have got such a detail wrong.

26. Sawyer, pp. 434 and 435. The charters mention the tombs of Æthelweard's two fallen sons, and are dated to December 937 – but the style is distinctively that of 'Athelstan A', and as it stands has almost certainly been tampered with by a forger.

27. William of Malmesbury, *Deeds of the Bishops of England*, trans. David Preest (Woodbridge: Boydell Press, 2002), p. 247.

28. *The Annals of Ulster*, entry for 939.

MALMESBURY

1. William of Malmesbury, 2.134.5.

2. Ibid., 1. *Prol.* 4.

3. Ibid., 2.132.

4. From the Exeter relic list; cited Conner, p. 177.

5. A letter from Radbod, Prior of Saint Samson, to Athelstan. Quoted by William of Malmesbury in *Deeds of the Bishops of England*, p. 249.

6. Byrhtferth, *Life of St Oswald*. Quoted by George Molyneaux, *The Formation of the English Kingdom in the Tenth Century* (Oxford: Oxford University Press, 2015), p. 212.

7. *Anglo-Saxon Chronicle* (D), entry for 973.

8. Henry of Huntingdon, 5.21. *The History of the English People, 1000–1154*, trans. D. E. Greenway (Oxford: Clarendon Press, 2002).

9. William of Malmesbury, 2.140.

10. Ibid., 2.132.

11. See Appendix 1 in Sarah Foot's biography of Athelstan for a summary of the latest scholarly thinking on the reliability or otherwise of William's claim to have found a lost biography of the king. 'William's account of Athelstan's life is a treacherous one . . . [but that he] had succeeded in finding a unique source of information about the king's reign seems certain; for that the biographer must express cautious gratitude' (p. 258). Readers interested in a more detailed – and positive – study of

William's reliability will have to wait for Michael Wood's *The Lost Life of King Aethelstan*, due out in spring 2017.

12. 'Battle of Brunanburh', 55.
13. Ibid., 9.
14. Æthelweard, 4.5.
15. William of Malmesbury, 2. *Prol.* 2.
16. 'King Edgar's Establishment of Monasteries', in *Councils and Synods, with Other Documents Relating to the English Church*, vol. 1: A.D. 871–1066, ed. D. Whitelock, M. Brett and C. N. L. Brooke (Oxford: Clarendon Press, 1982), p. 146.

Further Reading

To describe Sarah Foot's *Æthelstan: The First King of England* (New Haven and London: Yale University Press, 2011) as a biography would be overdoing it; but in so far as it is possible to write the standard life of so shadowy a figure, she has written it. Paul Hill's *The Age of Athelstan: Britain's Forgotten History* (Stroud: Tempus, 2004) provides a second, more readable book-length treatment of Athelstan's life and times.

Sir Frank Stenton's overview of the early medieval period, *Anglo-Saxon England* (Oxford: Oxford University Press, 1943), has long been rendered outdated by new finds and paradigms, but remains a classic, and gives a particularly detailed narrative of the rise of Wessex. Robin Fleming's *Britain After Rome: The Fall and Rise, 400 to 1070* (London: Allen Lane, 2010) provides an invaluable update. Another survey of early medieval England, also recent, similarly essential, is *The Anglo-Saxon World* (New Haven and London: Yale University Press, 2013), by Nicholas Higham and Martin Ryan. James Campbell's hugely influential series of essays on the precocity of the English state can be found in *Essays in Anglo-Saxon History* (London: Hambledon Press, 1986) and *The Anglo-Saxon State* (London: Hambledon and London, 2000). Michael Wood's *In Search of the Dark Ages* (London: Ariel, 1981) includes portraits of both Alfred and Athelstan, and is written with the same blend of scholarship and enthusiasm that has always made him Athelstan's most charismatic partisan.

Nicholas Higham's *The Kingdom of Northumbria, AD 350–1100* (Stroud: Alan Sutton, 1993) does what it says on the tin. *Mercia: The Anglo-Saxon Kingdom of Central England* (Woonton:

Logaston, 2001) by Sarah Zaluckyj provides a Midlands counter-point. The standard overview of Wessex is Barbara Yorke's *Wessex in the Early Middle Ages* (London: Leicester University Press, 1995), and is usefully complemented by David Dumville's collection of essays, *Wessex and England from Alfred to Edgar* (Woodbridge: Boydell Press, 1992). *Winchester in the Early Middle Ages*, edited by Martin Biddle (Oxford: Clarendon Press, 1976), provides a series of essays on the West Saxon capital.

The Anglo-Saxon sense – and indeed invention – of their past is stimulatingly explored in a range of surveys. Michael Hunter's 'Germanic and Roman Antiquity and the Sense of the Past in Anglo-Saxon England' (*Anglo-Saxon England* 3, 1974) traces how the fusion of Teutonic and classical influences on early medieval England came to be understood in the age of Alfred. A. L. Meaney's 'Woden in England: A Reconsideration of the Evidence' (*Folklore* 77, 1966) sheds a spotlight on Anglo-Saxon royal genealogies. Daniel Anlezark's 'Scæf, Japheth and the Origins of the Anglo-Saxons' (*Anglo-Saxon England* 31, 2002) and Rory Naismith's 'The Origins of the Line of Egbert, King of the West Saxons, 802–839' (*English Historical Review* 126, 2011) focus specifically on the lineage of the house of Wessex. H. E. Walker's 'Bede and the Gewissae: The Political Evolution of the Heptarchy and its Nomenclature' (*Cambridge Historical Journal* 12, 1956) is useful for tracing the evolution of West Saxon identity. Sarah Foot's two essays, 'The Making of *Angelcynn*: English Identity Before the Norman Conquest' (*Transactions of the Royal Historical Society* 6, 1996) and 'Remembering, Forgetting and Inventing: Attitudes to the Past in England at the End of the First Viking Age' (*Transactions of the Royal Historical Society* 9, 1999), provide twin overviews.

The political history of Wessex in the century before Athelstan's birth is traced by Richard Abels in 'Royal Succession and the Growth of Political Stability in Ninth-Century Wessex' (*Haskins Society Journal* 12, 2002), and by Simon Keynes in 'The Control of

Kent in the Ninth Century' (*Early Medieval Europe* 2, 1993). Richard Abels' *Alfred the Great: War, Kingship and Culture in Anglo-Saxon England* (London: Longman, 1998) is the standard biography of Athelstan's grandfather, while *Alfred the Great: Asser's Life of King Alfred and Other Contemporary Sources* (London: Penguin, 1983), edited by Simon Keynes and Michael Lapidge, ranks as very much more than an assemblage of the key primary sources for his reign. Keynes' 'King Alfred and the Mercians', in *Kings, Currency and Alliances: History and Coinage of Southern England in the Ninth Century*, edited by Mark A. S. Blackburn and David N. Dumville (Woodbridge: Boydell Press, 1998), focuses on the development of a self-consciously Anglo-Saxon identity. Janet Nelson's 'Power and Authority at the Court of Alfred', published in *Essays on Anglo-Saxon and Related Themes in Memory of Lynne Grundy*, edited by J. Roberts and J. L. Nelson (London: Centre for Late Antique and Medieval Studies, 2000), examines the ideology of kingship at Alfred's court.

The definitive survey of Edward's reign is provided by the collection of essays in *Edward the Elder* (London: Routledge, 2001), edited by Nicholas Higham and D. H. Hill. Ryan Lavelle's 'The Politics of Rebellion: The Ætheling Æthelwold and West Saxon Royal Succession, 899–902', in *Challenging the Boundaries of Medieval History: The Legacy of Timothy Reuter*, edited by Patricia Skinner (Turnhout: Brepols, 2009), surveys the issues at stake in Æthelwold's defiance of Edward. The best account of Æthelflæd's life remains F. T. Wainwright's 'Æthelflæd, Lady of the Mercians', in his highly readable collection of essays, *Scandinavian England: Collected Papers* (Chichester: Phillimore, 1975). Other studies of Æthelflæd include Pauline Stafford's ' "The Annals of Æthelflæd": Annals, History and Politics in Early Tenth-Century England', in *Myth, Rulership, Church and Charters*, edited by Julia Barrow and Andrew Wareham (Aldershot: Ashgate, 2007), and 'Æðelflæd of Mercia, *mise en page*', by Paul R. Szarmch, in *Words and Works: Studies in Medieval*

English Language and Literature in Honour of Fred C. Robinson, edited by Peter S. Baker and Nicholas Howe (Toronto: University of Toronto Press, 1998).

Like panners for gold, a number of scholars have focused on specific sources for the reign of Athelstan. Eric E. Barker's 'Two Lost Documents of King Athelstan' (*Anglo-Saxon England* 6, 1977) and Michael Lapidge's 'Some Latin Poems as Evidence for the Reign of Athelstan' (*Anglo-Saxon England* 9, 1980) both offer the thrill of the chase. The definitive survey of Athelstan's coronation ritual is Janet Nelson's 'The First Use of the Second Anglo-Saxon *Ordo*', in *Myth, Rulership, Church and Charters*, edited by Julia Barrow and Andrew Wareham (Aldershot: Ashgate, 2008). Michael Wood has written four essays which stirringly convey the sheer excitement of research into Athelstan's reign, and the fresh readings that can be garnered from it: 'The Making of King Æthelstan's Empire: An English Charlemagne?', in *Ideal and Reality in Frankish and Anglo-Saxon Society*, edited by P. Wormald (Oxford: Blackwell, 1983); 'The Lost Life of King Athelstan' and 'The Story of a Book', both published in *In Search of England: Journeys into the English Past* (London: Penguin, 1999); and '"Stand Strong Against the Monsters": Kingship and Learning in the Empire of King Æthelstan', in *Lay Intellectuals in the Carolingian World*, edited by Patrick Wormald and J. L. Nelson (Cambridge: Cambridge University Press, 2007).

A recent ground-breaking work on the emergence of an English kingdom in the tenth century, and what it meant for the rest of Britain, is George Molyneaux's *The Formation of the English Kingdom in the Tenth Century* (Oxford: Oxford University Press, 2015). Clare Downham's *Viking Kings of Britain and Ireland: The Dynasty of Ivarr to A.D. 1014* (Edinburgh: Dunedin Academic Press, 2007) provides the Scandinavian context for Athelstan's conquests, while Tim Clarkson's *Strathclyde and the Anglo-Saxons in the Viking Age* (Edinburgh: John Donald, 2014) is excellent on relations between the kingdoms of Wessex and Strathclyde. Dauvit Broun's *Scottish*

Independence and the Idea of Britain: From the Picts to Alexander III (Edinburgh: Edinburgh University Press, 2007) is invaluable for placing Athelstan's reign in the broader context of the emergence of the kingdoms of England and Scotland.

The definitive account of Athelstan's coinage is C. E. Blunt's 'The Coinage of Athelstan, 924–939: A Survey' (*British Numismatic Journal* 62, 1974). Additional detail can be found in Mark Blackburn's 'Mints, Burhs and the Grateley Code, Cap. 14.2', in *The Defence of Wessex: The Burghal Hidage and the Anglo-Saxon Fortifications*, edited by D. Hill and A. Rumble (Manchester: Manchester University Press, 1996). Athelstan's charters are catalogued in *Anglo-Saxon Charters: An Annotated List and Bibliography* (London: Royal Historical Society, 1968), edited by Peter Sawyer, and in *An Atlas of Attestations in Anglo-Saxon Charters, c.670–1066* (http://www.kemble.asnc.cam.ac.uk/node/30), compiled by Simon Keynes. Ben Snook's *The Anglo-Saxon Chancery: The History, Language and Production of Anglo-Saxon Charters from Alfred to Edgar* (Woodbridge: Boydell Press, 2015) is particularly useful on the enigmatic 'Athelstan A'. The Grateley Code is the focus of Ryan Lavelle's essay 'Why Grateley? Reflections on Anglo-Saxon Kingship in a Hampshire Landscape' (*Proceedings of the Hampshire Field Club and Archaeological Society* 60, 2005).

The life and afterlife of Saint Oswald are traced in the collection of essays edited by Clare Stancliffe and Eric Cambridge, *Oswald: Northumbrian King to European Saint* (Stamford: Paul Watkins, 1995). Athelstan's visit to Chester-le-Street boasts a starring role in *St Cuthbert, his Cult and his Community to AD 1200*, edited by Gerald Bonner, David Rollason and Clare Stancliffe (Woodbridge: Boydell Press, 1989). Mechtild Gretsch's *Ælfric and the Cult of Saints in Late Anglo-Saxon England* (Cambridge: Cambridge University Press, 2009) provides a useful context for studying Athelstan's devotion to relics.

Paul Hill's *The Anglo-Saxons at War 800–1066* (Barnsley: Pen & Sword Military, 2012) provides a valuable overview of warfare in the late Anglo-Saxon period, while *The Defence of Wessex* (op. cit.) focuses specifically on the fortifications built by Alfred and his successors. Neil Price's *The Viking Way* (Uppsala: Uppsala University Press, 2002) is thrilling on Viking warfare, and R. G. Poole's *Viking Poems on War and Peace: A Study in Skaldic Narrative* (Toronto: Toronto University Press, 1991) provides a useful complement. Predatory beasts stalk the pages of both Alexander Pluskowski's *Wolves and the Wilderness in the Middle Ages* (Woodbridge: Boydell Press, 2006) and Mohamed Eric Rahman Lacey's fascinating PhD thesis, 'Birds and Bird-lore in the Literature of Anglo-Saxon England'. A stirring overview of the theme of animals in warrior culture is provided by Thomas Williams' essay, ' "For the Sake of Bravado in the Wilderness": Confronting the Bestial in Anglo-Saxon Warfare', in *Representing Beasts in Early Medieval England and Scandinavia*, edited by Michael Bintley and Thomas Williams (Woodbridge: Boydell Press, 2015).

That the mystery of Brunanburh's location is ultimately unsolvable has not prevented numerous historians of Athelstan's reign from attempting to provide a definitive answer. Michael Livingstone's *The Battle of Brunanburh: A Casebook* (Exeter: University of Exeter Press, 2011) provides sterling service by assembling all the sources for the battle in a single book; nevertheless, its argument that Brunanburh is to be identified with Bromborough in the Wirral is too tendentiously made to be convincing. Also pressing the case for Bromborough is J. McN. Dodgson in 'The Background of Brunanburh' (*Saga-Book of the Viking Society* XIV, 1953–7) and Nicholas Higham in 'The Context of Brunanburh', in *Names, Places and People: An Onomastic Miscellany in Memory of John McNeal Dodgson*, edited by A. R. Rumble and A. D. Mills (Stamford: Paul Watkins, 1997). Michael Wood's essay 'Brunanburh Revisited' (*Saga-Book of the Viking Society* XX, 1978–80) argues for the battle having been fought near the Humber on the frontier of Mercia and Northumbria; a case which he then refines in 'Tinsley Wood', in *In*

Search of England: Journeys into the English Past (London: Penguin, 1999). Kevin Halloran in 'The Brunanburh Campaign: A Reappraisal' (*Scottish Historical Review* 84, 2005) argues for Burnswark in Annandale.

For Athelstan's successors, see Pauline Stafford's *Unification and Conquest: A Political and Social History of England in the Tenth and Eleventh Centuries* (London: Edward Arnold, 1989).

Picture Credits

1. Alfred the Great: silver penny, ninth century (© The Trustees of the British Museum, London, BM 1915,0507.798)
2. The Alfred Jewel: gold, rock crystal and enamel, ninth century (Ashmolean Museum, University of Oxford/Bridgeman Images)
3. Edward the Elder: silver pseudo-coin brooch, early tenth century (© The Trustees of the British Museum, London, BM 1951,0206.1)
4. Statue of the young Athelstan with his aunt, Æthelflæd, 1913, at Tamworth Castle, Staffordshire (Alamy)
5. The ruins of Saint Oswald's Priory, c. 900, Gloucester (Alamy)
6. Coin from Æthelflæd's mint in Chester depicting a tower, early tenth century (Author collection/James Muir)
7. The coronation stone, Kingston upon Thames (Alamy)
8. Coin from Athelstan's York mint, possibly depicting York Minster, tenth century (Author collection/James Muir)
9. Frontispiece to Bede's *Life of St Cuthbert*, showing Athelstan presenting the book to Saint Cuthbert, c. 934 (The Master and Fellows of Corpus Christi College, Cambridge, MS 183, f.1v)
10. Hebrews with their livestock: miniature from the Junius (or Caedmon) manuscript, tenth century (De Agostini Picture Library/Bridgeman Images)
11. Detail from a stole placed in Saint Cuthbert's tomb by Athelstan, embroidered with the name of Ælfflæd, early tenth century (By kind permission of the Chapter of Durham Cathedral)
12. *The Royal Couple (Herrscherpaar)*, c.1250, wooden figures thought to show Otto the Great and his wife Eadgyth, in Magdeburg Cathedral, Germany (Alamy)

13. Miniature showing Christ in Majesty, from the Athelstan Psalter, second quarter of the tenth century (British Library, Cotton MS Galba A XVIII fol. 2v/Bridgeman Images)

14. Silver coin of Athelstan, stamped '*REX TO BR*', tenth century (© The Trustees of the British Museum, London, BM 1955,0708.46)

15. Athelstan's tomb, fifteenth century, in Malmesbury Abbey, Wiltshire (Alamy)

Index

Penguin Monarchs

THE HOUSES OF WESSEX AND DENMARK

Athelstan*	Tom Holland
Aethelred the Unready	Richard Abels
Cnut	Ryan Lavelle
Edward the Confessor	

THE HOUSES OF NORMANDY, BLOIS AND ANJOU

William I*	Marc Morris
William II	John Gillingham
Henry I	Edmund King
Stephen	Carl Watkins
Henry II*	Richard Barber
Richard I	Thomas Asbridge
John	Nicholas Vincent

THE HOUSE OF PLANTAGENET

Henry III	Stephen Church
Edward I*	Andy King
Edward II	Christopher Given-Wilson
Edward III*	Jonathan Sumption
Richard II*	Laura Ashe

THE HOUSES OF LANCASTER AND YORK

Henry IV	Catherine Nall
Henry V*	Anne Curry
Henry VI	James Ross
Edward IV	A. J. Pollard
Edward V	Thomas Penn
Richard III	Rosemary Horrox

* Now in paperback

THE HOUSE OF TUDOR

Henry VII   Sean Cunningham
Henry VIII*   John Guy
Edward VI*   Stephen Alford
Mary I*   John Edwards
Elizabeth I   Helen Castor

THE HOUSE OF STUART

James I   Thomas Cogswell
Charles I*   Mark Kishlansky
[Cromwell*   David Horspool]
Charles II*   Clare Jackson
James II   David Womersley
William III & Mary II*   Jonathan Keates
Anne   Richard Hewlings

THE HOUSE OF HANOVER

George I   Tim Blanning
George II   Norman Davies
George III   Amanda Foreman
George IV   Stella Tillyard
William IV   Roger Knight
Victoria*   Jane Ridley

THE HOUSES OF SAXE-COBURG & GOTHA AND WINDSOR

Edward VII*   Richard Davenport-Hines
George V*   David Cannadine
Edward VIII*   Piers Brendon
George VI*   Philip Ziegler
Elizabeth II*   Douglas Hurd

* Now in paperback

ALLEN LANE
an imprint of
PENGUIN BOOKS

Also Published

Stephen Kotkin, *Stalin, Vol. II: Waiting for Hitler, 1928-1941*

Lindsey Fitzharris, *The Butchering Art: Joseph Lister's Quest to Transform the Grisly World of Victorian Medicine*

Serhii Plokhy, *Lost Kingdom: A History of Russian Nationalism from Ivan the Great to Vladimir Putin*

Mark Mazower, *What You Did Not Tell: A Russian Past and the Journey Home*

Lawrence Freedman, *The Future of War: A History*

Niall Ferguson, *The Square and the Tower: Networks, Hierarchies and the Struggle for Global Power*

Matthew Walker, *Why We Sleep: The New Science of Sleep and Dreams*

Edward O. Wilson, *The Origins of Creativity*

John Bradshaw, *The Animals Among Us: The New Science of Anthropology*

David Cannadine, *Victorious Century: The United Kingdom, 1800-1906*

Leonard Susskind and Art Friedman, *Special Relativity and Classical Field Theory*

Maria Alyokhina, *Riot Days*

Oona A. Hathaway and Scott J. Shapiro, *The Internationalists: And Their Plan to Outlaw War*

Chris Renwick, *Bread for All: The Origins of the Welfare State*

Anne Applebaum, *Red Famine: Stalin's War on Ukraine*

Richard McGregor, *Asia's Reckoning: The Struggle for Global Dominance*

Chris Kraus, *After Kathy Acker: A Biography*

Clair Wills, *Lovers and Strangers: An Immigrant History of Post-War Britain*

Odd Arne Westad, *The Cold War: A World History*

Max Tegmark, *Life 3.0: Being Human in the Age of Artificial Intelligence*

Jonathan Losos, *Improbable Destinies: How Predictable is Evolution?*

Chris D. Thomas, *Inheritors of the Earth: How Nature Is Thriving in an Age of Extinction*

Chris Patten, *First Confession: A Sort of Memoir*

James Delbourgo, *Collecting the World: The Life and Curiosity of Hans Sloane*

Naomi Klein, *No Is Not Enough: Defeating the New Shock Politics*

Ulrich Raulff, *Farewell to the Horse: The Final Century of Our Relationship*

Slavoj Žižek, *The Courage of Hopelessness: Chronicles of a Year of Acting Dangerously*

Patricia Lockwood, *Priestdaddy: A Memoir*

Ian Johnson, *The Souls of China: The Return of Religion After Mao*

Stephen Alford, *London's Triumph: Merchant Adventurers and the Tudor City*

Hugo Mercier and Dan Sperber, *The Enigma of Reason: A New Theory of Human Understanding*

Stuart Hall, *Familiar Stranger: A Life Between Two Islands*

Allen Ginsberg, *The Best Minds of My Generation: A Literary History of the Beats*

Sayeeda Warsi, *The Enemy Within: A Tale of Muslim Britain*

Alexander Betts and Paul Collier, *Refuge: Transforming a Broken Refugee System*

Robert Bickers, *Out of China: How the Chinese Ended the Era of Western Domination*

Erica Benner, *Be Like the Fox: Machiavelli's Lifelong Quest for Freedom*

William D. Cohan, *Why Wall Street Matters*

David Horspool, *Oliver Cromwell: The Protector*

Daniel C. Dennett, *From Bacteria to Bach and Back: The Evolution of Minds*

Derek Thompson, *Hit Makers: How Things Become Popular*

Harriet Harman, *A Woman's Work*

Wendell Berry, *The World-Ending Fire: The Essential Wendell Berry*

Daniel Levin, *Nothing but a Circus: Misadventures among the Powerful*

Stephen Church, *Henry III: A Simple and God-Fearing King*

Pankaj Mishra, *Age of Anger: A History of the Present*

Graeme Wood, *The Way of the Strangers: Encounters with the Islamic State*

Michael Lewis, *The Undoing Project: A Friendship that Changed the World*

John Romer, *A History of Ancient Egypt, Volume 2: From the Great Pyramid to the Fall of the Middle Kingdom*

Andy King, *Edward I: A New King Arthur?*

Thomas L. Friedman, *Thank You for Being Late: An Optimist's Guide to Thriving in the Age of Accelerations*

John Edwards, *Mary I: The Daughter of Time*

Grayson Perry, *The Descent of Man*

Deyan Sudjic, *The Language of Cities*

Norman Ohler, *Blitzed: Drugs in Nazi Germany*

Carlo Rovelli, *Reality Is Not What It Seems: The Journey to Quantum Gravity*

Catherine Merridale, *Lenin on the Train*

Susan Greenfield, *A Day in the Life of the Brain: The Neuroscience of Consciousness from Dawn Till Dusk*

Christopher Given-Wilson, *Edward II: The Terrors of Kingship*

Emma Jane Kirby, *The Optician of Lampedusa*

Minoo Dinshaw, *Outlandish Knight: The Byzantine Life of Steven Runciman*

Candice Millard, *Hero of the Empire: The Making of Winston Churchill*

Christopher de Hamel, *Meetings with Remarkable Manuscripts*

Brian Cox and Jeff Forshaw, *Universal: A Guide to the Cosmos*

Ryan Avent, *The Wealth of Humans: Work and Its Absence in the Twenty-first Century*

Jodie Archer and Matthew L. Jockers, *The Bestseller Code*

Cathy O'Neil, *Weapons of Math Destruction: How Big Data Increases Inequality and Threatens Democracy*

Peter Wadhams, *A Farewell to Ice: A Report from the Arctic*

Richard J. Evans, *The Pursuit of Power: Europe, 1815-1914*

Anthony Gottlieb, *The Dream of Enlightenment: The Rise of Modern Philosophy*

Marc Morris, *William I: England's Conqueror*

Gareth Stedman Jones, *Karl Marx: Greatness and Illusion*

J.C.H. King, *Blood and Land: The Story of Native North America*

Robert Gerwarth, *The Vanquished: Why the First World War Failed to End, 1917-1923*

Joseph Stiglitz, *The Euro: And Its Threat to Europe*

John Bradshaw and Sarah Ellis, *The Trainable Cat: How to Make Life Happier for You and Your Cat*

A J Pollard, *Edward IV: The Summer King*

Erri de Luca, *The Day Before Happiness*

Diarmaid MacCulloch, *All Things Made New: Writings on the Reformation*

Daniel Beer, *The House of the Dead: Siberian Exile Under the Tsars*

Tom Holland, *Athelstan: The Making of England*

Christopher Goscha, *The Penguin History of Modern Vietnam*

Mark Singer, *Trump and Me*

Roger Scruton, *The Ring of Truth: The Wisdom of Wagner's Ring of the Nibelung*

Ruchir Sharma, *The Rise and Fall of Nations: Ten Rules of Change in the Post-Crisis World*

Jonathan Sumption, *Edward III: A Heroic Failure*

Daniel Todman, *Britain's War: Into Battle, 1937-1941*

Dacher Keltner, *The Power Paradox: How We Gain and Lose Influence*

Tom Gash, *Criminal: The Truth About Why People Do Bad Things*

Brendan Simms, *Britain's Europe: A Thousand Years of Conflict and Cooperation*

Slavoj Žižek, *Against the Double Blackmail: Refugees, Terror, and Other Troubles with the Neighbours*

Lynsey Hanley, *Respectable: The Experience of Class*

Piers Brendon, *Edward VIII: The Uncrowned King*

Matthew Desmond, *Evicted: Poverty and Profit in the American City*

T.M. Devine, *Independence or Union: Scotland's Past and Scotland's Present*

Seamus Murphy, *The Republic*

Jerry Brotton, *This Orient Isle: Elizabethan England and the Islamic World*

Srinath Raghavan, *India's War: The Making of Modern South Asia, 1939-1945*

Clare Jackson, *Charles II: The Star King*

Nandan Nilekani and Viral Shah, *Rebooting India: Realizing a Billion Aspirations*

Sunil Khilnani, *Incarnations: India in 50 Lives*

Helen Pearson, *The Life Project: The Extraordinary Story of Our Ordinary Lives*

Ben Ratliff, *Every Song Ever: Twenty Ways to Listen to Music Now*

Richard Davenport-Hines, *Edward VII: The Cosmopolitan King*

Peter H. Wilson, *The Holy Roman Empire: A Thousand Years of Europe's History*

Todd Rose, *The End of Average: How to Succeed in a World that Values Sameness*

Frank Trentmann, *Empire of Things: How We Became a World of Consumers, from the Fifteenth Century to the Twenty-First*

Laura Ashe, *Richard II: A Brittle Glory*

John Donvan and Caren Zucker, *In a Different Key: The Story of Autism*

Jack Shenker, *The Egyptians: A Radical Story*

Tim Judah, *In Wartime: Stories from Ukraine*

Serhii Plokhy, *The Gates of Europe: A History of Ukraine*

Robin Lane Fox, *Augustine: Conversions and Confessions*

Peter Hennessy and James Jinks, *The Silent Deep: The Royal Navy Submarine Service Since 1945*

Sean McMeekin, *The Ottoman Endgame: War, Revolution and the Making of the Modern Middle East, 1908–1923*

Charles Moore, *Margaret Thatcher: The Authorized Biography, Volume Two: Everything She Wants*

Dominic Sandbrook, *The Great British Dream Factory: The Strange History of Our National Imagination*

Larissa MacFarquhar, *Strangers Drowning: Voyages to the Brink of Moral Extremity*

Niall Ferguson, *Kissinger: 1923-1968: The Idealist*

Carlo Rovelli, *Seven Brief Lessons on Physics*

Tim Blanning, *Frederick the Great: King of Prussia*

Ian Kershaw, *To Hell and Back: Europe, 1914–1949*

Pedro Domingos, *The Master Algorithm: How the Quest for the Ultimate Learning Machine Will Remake Our World*

David Wootton, *The Invention of Science: A New History of the Scientific Revolution*